One of Austr[a]... actors, and a veteran of film, television and theatre, Steve Bisley has been performing since the late seventies. A two-times winner of the AFI award for Best Supporting Actor and a member of the Australian Film Walk of Fame, Steve is now turning his hand to writing. *Stillways*, a memoir, is his first published work.

STEVE BISLEY

Stillways

A MEMOIR

FOURTH ESTATE

Fourth Estate
An imprint of HarperCollins*Publishers*

First published in Australia in 2013
by HarperCollins*Publishers* Australia Pty Limited
ABN 36 009 913 517
harpercollins.com.au

Copyright © Steve Bisley 2013

The right of Steve Bisley to be identified as the author of this work has been asserted by him in accordance with the *Copyright Amendment (Moral Rights) Act 2000*.

This work is copyright. Apart from any use as permitted under the *Copyright Act 1968*, no part may be reproduced, copied, scanned, stored in a retrieval system, recorded, or transmitted, in any form or by any means, without the prior written permission of the publisher.

HarperCollins*Publishers*
Level 13, 201 Elizabeth Street, Sydney NSW 2000, Australia
31 View Road, Glenfield, Auckland 0627, New Zealand
A 53, Sector 57, Noida, UP, India
77–85 Fulham Palace Road, London W6 8JB, United Kingdom
2 Bloor Street East, 20th floor, Toronto, Ontario M4W 1A8, Canada
10 East 53rd Street, New York NY 10022, USA

Bisley, Steve.
  Stillways : a memoir / Steve Bisley.
  978 0 7322 9784 8 (paperback)
  978 1 4607 0035 8 (ebook)
  Bisley, Steve.
  Actors – Australia – Biography.
792.028092

Cover design by Philip Campbell Design
Cover images: Childhood photo of Steve Bisley courtesy Steve Bisley; background image by Megan Czisz
Author photo: Jimmy Malecki
Typeset in Baskerville MT by Kirby Jones
Printed and bound in Australia by Griffin Press
The papers used by HarperCollins in the manufacture of this book are natural, recyclable products made from wood grown in sustainable plantation forests. The fibre source and manufacturing processes meet recognised international environmental standards, and carry certification.

7 6 5 4   13 14 15 16

For Krissie

The soaking wind curves around the channel that empties Lake Macquarie into the Pacific Ocean. It blows across Pulbah Island and reaches to the sodden south. There is no rain, but a thin wetness. There is no whisper through the casuarinas brought by other winds; they are bowed and heavy now and all things feel sunk and riven.

This is the only way to see my home. This is the only true way to see my home.

We could walk from the creek to the house, on other days, when the bright nor'easter sang through the big gums and sifted the green paddocks. I could show you the pump house by the creek. We could start the big diesel and feel the irrigation lines throb and fatten and see the monsoon sprinklers throw their fine rainbows of misty water skywards.

But best not to.

Best tell it like it was.

Rather we should wait beside the pump-house shed. It won't be long.

Look, here he comes! Look, there – up the track that runs between the two fenced paddocks!

That's him!

That's my father!

He's a long way off, but even through the wet mist you can see the purpose in him.

He has a small sack in his hand that swings as he walks and even at this distance you can hear the kittens crying.

Swing …

Swing …

Inside the sack, a brick and some kittens.

He walks past where we are standing.

Plop!

Splash!

Inside the sack, a brick and some kittens. And water.

Down, down to the countless sacks.

He will walk back to the house now; remove his boots, sit in his place at the head of the table, and drink.

Drink long and deep from the longnecks.

And no one will disturb him.

Rather we will wait in the sodden yard till this communion is over.

The mother and the ducklings.

'Hush now! Your father's had a hard day.'

In the failing light I watch the few cows blow steam from their noses. The mist lies heavily on their broad backs as they eat themselves forward. They eat themselves forward all day. They do nothing else but eat.

Eat, forward, eat, forward, eat, forward.

We wait; it's always the same, this ritual.

There is a man sitting alone at a table inside a house. Drinking.

Outside is a woman with three children. Waiting.

We will go in, after a while.

When we do, we will each go to our rooms in the dark house to sit and learn to be lonely. We will sit with the sadness of our father, till it takes hold and never leaves us.

Stillways

We lived at the end of Carter's Road.

It dived off the Pacific Highway at Lake Munmorah, midway between Wyong and Swansea, on the Central Coast of New South Wales.

The road got its name from the Carter family, our next-door neighbours. They were orchardists with the biggest farm in the area, so they got the road named after them.

My father had cut our farm out of virgin bush after the Second World War. It was only fifteen acres. He had built the house with the help of local men. There was also a shed, and two fenced paddocks running from the shed to a creek. Apart from some yards used to pen the few head of cattle and our various horses and a chicken coop, there wasn't much else.

There were other farms along Carter's Road – smallholdings, like ours.

The Nickelsons, who were horsey; Mrs Tillock, the widow; a family of Jehovah's Witnesses called Dickie; and the Carters of course.

I'm Stephen – or Stevie, because I'm the youngest.

My sister, Kristin, is three years older than me, my brother, Richard, is two years older than her.

My mother's name is Pauline.

She is unloved by my father.

My father's name is Bruce.

There was always work to do at home.

Blokes on bulldozers tore down the lovely gums. The once smooth and silken trunks fell to the earth shrieking, gashed and splintered from the blade.

Once down, they were pushed together and heaped to burn for days, the air sweet with the smell of eucalypt, bleeding sap and diesel.

After the machines had left, us kids would come and start the stick picking. Days bent over, picking up the broken branches, root ends and leaves to hurl them onto the fires.

Then back came the bulldozers to push again and again, year after year, till finally we set the boundaries of our lives with taut wire fences.

Stillways, our farm.

My parents were market gardeners before they gave it away to become schoolteachers. It always seemed to me that when they had made the shift they had just gone from one group of vegetables to another.

I remember running down the rows of ripe tomatoes; at the end of each row, you fairly reeked. I loved the smell. It stuck to you and stayed. When you bit them they slushed in your mouth and after you swallowed, the taste hung there for hours.

We grew vegies for market. Tomatoes, beans, watermelons and pumpkins.

They were sorted in the shed, loaded on Fridays and trucked to the market in Newcastle.

I would curl up on the springy seat of the old Dodge truck in the predawn as my father nursed our way north on the Pacific Highway.

At the markets, men in cracked leather aprons with large wads of money slid the greasy notes sidewards to my father. 'Can't give you much, Bruce, just got too many of 'em to shift. You know what it's like.'

He didn't.

He wore the disappointment like another skin. You could see it visibly take him, and when it did, it consumed him, and the black rage would rise.

I tried to tell him that I was sorry.

Sorry that his work had earnt so little.

But there was nothing between us that would let me in.

I knew why he took me with him.

He needed someone to witness the wrong he felt.

To save him from the darkness within.

We rode back south, me and him, through the wakening suburbs of Newcastle, past the blackened port where tugs nudged the empty ships under the hulking coal loader and more waited in the inky blue to load and go.

Newcastle had coal under it a mile deep. The flinty black seams of it ran up and down the coast forever. There wasn't a village within cooee of it that didn't have its own pit. Our farm was twenty-five miles from the heart of Newcastle, but even at that distance we knew there were men deep beneath our paddocks toiling at the coalface.

On the southern outskirts of the city the road narrowed to the coast.

Dad down-shifted through the whiny gearbox and eased the truck over the rickety Swansea Bridge to park in front of the pub.

'I'll be an hour,' he said. 'Stay out of trouble!'

The pub was an early opener and even at eight am on a Saturday it was crowded. Miners, off shift, propped up the bar with farmers, tradies and fishermen. Blokes in pork-pie hats studied the racing form and blowsy women shrieked over the din. There was a gaggle of kids on the footpath waiting, forbidden to stray, caught in the draught of hop-sweet air and smoke from the saloon.

I left the truck, its motor tick-ticking as the engine cooled, and headed back to the bridge.

Past the newsagent with its inky smell of paper and titty cards bending in racks on the footpath: *Having the breast time in Swansea. Wish you were here!*

Bags of green plastic soldiers half price out the front. Wishing I had a bob for a roll of caps, just for the smell of them after the bang.

Further up, the cake shop, opening now. Fat lamingtons, cream horns, horseshoes and pies. Pavlova in the window with a fly on the fruit.

Wish I had another bob.

The fire station with the limp hoses hoisted on poles and the big truck, polished, gleaming red in the cool inside.

The squat police station where Jimmy Evans, the local copper, dealt out justice with a heavy hand.

There are houses with beachy shells stuck to their front walls. Bleached shacks with names like Bide A While, Shangri-la and Mick's Palace.

Tanned people lounge in their front yards on some permanent holiday.

Loony gnomes peer out from the barren cacti gardens.

A white cocky in a cage with its lemony crest unfurled screeches. 'Ricky!'

On the bridge, blokes bend over the railing, staring into the blue-green spiralling eddies for the flash of silver. Gulls overhead on wings that shape the fresh nor'easter to keep them held above us. Fish scales and gull crap.

The bridge spans the channel that draws the rolling greenies from the Pacific Ocean and funnels them across the bar to freshen the lake.

I let the time pass; an hour, he said. I know he will be drinking deeply in the pub now, brooding, dark and dangerous.

I stay on the bridge in the clean brightness.

I am scared to go back.

I don't know what I'll find.

I don't know how he'll be.

We never know.

Until it's too late.

I wait on the bridge, and hope.

I am windblown and bleached and too small for this.

Finally I head back to the pub. I wait quietly in the truck until he comes, the smell of dirt and beer is all over him. We'll drive home now, unload, and I'll join the others in a paddock of sticks.

*

Later that day, Dad accuses me of swearing at my brother and orders me to wait in the shed. So now it comes. Usually we have to pick our own stick to be beaten with, but today Dad has one with him when he arrives.

He lays into the backs of my legs. I can smell his breath, still beery from the pub, as he thrashes me, and I know this is not really about my behaviour; it's about the price of fruit.

A day in my life

We didn't have electricity. Everyone else in the district had the power on, but not down our road. We had the poles – they'd been there for years, greying and split – but nothing else. My father had wired the house in anticipation of our connection to the grid but we remained dark and dim. We had kerosene lamps and a wood-burning stove to cook on. One of my jobs was to make sure there was always enough wood for the kitchen and the big open fire that warmed the house in winter. I split the sawn logs on a big block beside the shed. I gathered bundles of kindling. I was young and determined.

We had Aladdin lamps to light our house at night. At dusk my mother would gather the lamps and set them on the kitchen table. She would fill them with the blue kerosene, trim the wicks, light them and set their tall glass chimneys in place.

We spent our nights in the soft glow of them. It made the whole house seem like a shrine to something, as if we'd invoked something holy.

In winter, when the open fire in the lounge room was burning, I would sit for hours in front of it, caught by the mystery of the dancing flames and the deep, deep core of it.

At bedtime we would take small lamps into our rooms. They had sand in the bottom to stop them from falling over. I would lie in my small bed with the shadows dancing on the walls and the big house settling. Frogs bongoed from the creek, flying foxes in leathery squadrons screeched through the orchard, possums skidded on the iron roof. There was the faraway sound of a train and, faintly, the mopokes hunting in the dark bush.

In the morning the house lifts gently on its stumps as the dawn gathers.

The five bodies of my family come to life with the last thoughts of the night slithering back and further back, and for the briefest moment we are as one, together but alone.

*

Mornings are busy. There's the kitchen stove to be stoked and readied for the rush. Wood shoved into the firebox, toast burnt on the open flames, eggs knocking together in a blackened saucepan, thick porridge ladled out with golden syrup swirled through.

I brush my beaten school shoes with a double beat on the front verandah; my toes are curled against the cold as I watch the roos invade the paddocks in the dew.

My brother, Richard, who is older, cuffs me under the ear on his way to the outside dunny, slams the door and rips a great fart into the morning. The dunny doesn't flush; it slowly fills over a week to be taken away by the dunny man, who leaves an empty one in its place. At Christmas time my father leaves a bottle of beer by the front gate. It's a gift to the dunny man for taking our shit away for a whole year.

I've only recently learnt to swear.

Some kid told me that he saw the dunny man eating his lunch and he dropped an apple into one of the full cans of shit and he just reached in and got the apple out, wiped it on his shitty pants and ate it! I didn't believe it.

I wondered if the dunny man ever got really clean and had a wife who really loved him.

On his way back from the dunny my brother cuffs me under the other ear. He doesn't know that he's my hero, but then again, I'm my sister's boyfriend too and she doesn't know that either.

I've got lots of secrets.

I'm a watcher.

I know where my father hides his condoms! They're in a white box in the third drawer down in a cupboard in my parents' bedroom, right beside his large Y-fronted undies. I don't know what I was looking for when I found them; I think I was just having a general look around, digging for other people's secrets to make them my own.

So my parents were having sex!

Right!

Some nights I creep from my bed and glide like a shadow into the lounge room and wait. Wait for the slightest sound of proof. The rustle of a sheet, a sigh or the sound of a body shifting. In the mornings I look for the telltale signs of the night's coupling, but there are never any. Or maybe there are and I don't know what I'm looking for. There is something going on because my father gets through a lot of condoms; I know, I check them every week.

I didn't know much about sex, only that it required some form of rubbing.

I did know, most years, where my parents hid the Christmas presents.

That my sister hid beans in the side of her mouth at dinnertime and, unseen, spat them out through the bathroom window into the garden.

That my brother had a book with pictures of girls' boobies under his bed.

I slide my books into my satchel and find my lunch on the kitchen bench. My school bag smells of banana and pencils. Then we're all out the door together. Us kids will walk the half-mile up Carter's Road to catch the school bus at the highway. I want to walk close to Richard 'cause he smells of Brylcreem. He is square and muscled and handsome, in his last year at high school now, and all he wants is to be a farmer. Mum walks with us. She teaches at a small school at the end of our road. My sister, Kris, is with us too, all pigtails and whip-smart.

Back at home my father eases the big black Jaguar from the carport. Inside it smells of women and my father. It has walnut wood carved into a dashboard and silver vases for cut flowers above the back seat. It has courtesy lights and a lighter with CIGAR printed on its black knob and a jaguar's head that stares out from the centre of a silver-spoked steering wheel. There is an ashtray that slides out from under the dashboard. Inside it are cigarette butts with fresh red lipstick on them.

Like I said, I'm a watcher.

We are halfway to the highway when the Jaguar catches us. We stand to one side of the gravel road as Dad glides by in his lovely car. He is going to another school to teach strangers the things he can't teach us.

My father has more secrets than me.

I wait beside the Pacific Highway. It's as big as its name. Its blue-black surface goes forever, or at least to Queensland. There's a mob of kids in the bus shelter now, but I want to wait right here, beside the highway's edge. There's life in these cars, bold stuff flashing by me.

Blonde woman, red mouth, with a guy slumped and leaning on her shoulder. Man in a suit with his hand on his forehead. An older woman driving with a neat man in the passenger seat, both peering ahead into the morning.

The school bus looms into a close-up and drags me back from wherever and I'm right in a fight for the door and a seat by the window. Daryl Carter slides in beside me; he's my neighbour, but whatever he's got to say can wait, 'cause I'm still with the blonde in the Chevy. Daryl fidgets beside me. He's such a kid; he's only nine.

Still, I tell him about the Elvis Presley movie we saw with my parents at the drive-in on Friday. Daryl wants to know what Elvis sang. I lose interest and drift back to the road. Daddy-o!

It's 1962 and on Boxing Day I'll be twelve.

Daryl and me and the other primary kids get off at Kanwal for our school.

The bus pulls away with the high-school kids to take them to Wyong.

I get a flash of my sister, who smiles down at me, and further along Richard squashes his face into the windowpane and leers. 'Shithead!'

It takes me till lunchtime to get Elvis out of my head but the blonde lingers. She has wet pink lipstick and she dances like crazy.

In the playground, we play handball and drink warm milk. I miss an easy put-away shot and drift away to the boys' toilets, to be alone. I catch a glimpse of me in the mirrors above the hand basins and, although I don't know it then, I'm watching the boy in me begin to fade.

In the afternoon we draw numbers out of a hat to see who we will partner at our end-of-year social – our last dance in primary school. The girls already have a number. The boys all want Susan Green. She is number six. I reach into the hat, my hand begins to tremble and my face feels hot and scratchy. My mates are chanting, 'Number six! Number six!' I look up, straight into the blue eyes of Susan Green. I open my hand. Bingo!

Later that day we have dance practice in the school hall. I think I love Susan Green because my face gets hot when I look at her and something makes my legs shake. We meet briefly in the Barn Dance when she swirls towards me and clasps my hand in hers. She smells like a promise.

Later I ride home on the school bus. I hear the babble of kids all around me, but all I can think about is her. I am totally, utterly in love.

I get off the bus and walk the half-mile home down Carter's Road. Mum's in the kitchen when I arrive and there is another woman there having afternoon tea. Mum says, 'Mrs Coombs' daughter needs a partner for the social and I told her that I'm sure you'd be delighted to take her.'

The reason Mrs Coombs' daughter, Jane, needs a partner for the social is that she is the fattest, ugliest girl in the school – no, make that the universe.

Mum excuses us then leads me into the lounge room out of Mrs Coombs' earshot. She draws me close to her, which is rare. 'Now, you know that little Jane lost her father early this year, and I think it would be great if you could take her to the social. Mrs Coombs says that Jane admires you and would love it if you would partner her. What do you say?'

What do I say? I could say I'm already partnering the best-looking girl in the school to the social. I could say that I'm so in love with her that if I don't take her to the social

I might actually die! I could say that if you make me take a baby elephant to the social, I might leave home and never come back.

What do I say? I say sure, I'll take Jane. Why? Because of the way I've been raised. Mum says I am generous of spirit. Mum tells Mrs Coombs the news. Mrs Coombs is overjoyed and envelops me in a fat embrace. She is fat and sweaty, just like Jane, my new date, the girl who admires me.

A week later, on the last day of primary school, we are packing up our belongings and clearing out our desks when it settles on me that this is the end of the first chapter of the book of my life. At lunchtime I take a curling sandwich from my bag and head up the hill behind the cricket pitch for a last look.

Down below, it all looks suddenly small, like I've outgrown it. Like a snakeskin that's been discarded for the new one underneath. There's the weather shed where we'd run to when it rained; the handball court with the fading lines; the neat classrooms where we grew and learnt so much. I took a marble from my pocket and buried it where I sat so that a piece of me stayed there like a memory.

I told Susan Green what had happened between the mothers. She said she understood, but I knew she didn't, not really.

I took Jane to the social.

I made sure she had a good time because Mum was right: I was generous of spirit. I watched Susan across the room with her new partner. I felt the loss somewhere deep inside and it really hurt. It hurt so much!

It was sewn into your skin, this first love, like all the other firsts; like breath, like food, like warmth. It stayed.

I had bought Susan some makeup from Coles with my pocket money. Lipstick, eye shadow, mascara and a lot of other mysterious stuff. I got a whole brown paper bag full for ten bob. I'd carried the brown paper bag around for a week, trying to find the right time to give it to her, but finally I was too embarrassed, too scared.

On that very last day of primary school, as the buses lined up to take us home, I fought my way through a wall of kids onto her bus to find her. I thrust the now soiled bag at her and blurted out the words 'I like you'. I stumbled off the bus, my face flushed red from the ordeal, and lost myself in the crowd. She went to a different high school from me. I hoped she liked the present. I hoped she liked me.

Summer

I could always just hold out for summer and the Christmas school holidays. This was my last holiday before high school. I didn't know if I was ready for big school; I didn't know what it would be like. It worried me, the unknown bit.

But I had six weeks of the summer break before then, with Christmas and my birthday to look forward to. Most days we headed to the creek. It ran from the bottom of the paddocks and snaked its way past the stands of paper barks and river gums to the reedy northern borders of the farm, to finally tip into the southern end of Lake Macquarie. My father had dammed the section below the paddocks and pumped the salty water out till, over time, it filled with fresh water for irrigation.

We would head to the salty side below the dam wall to fish and swim. We made rude canoes out of corrugated iron and filled the open ends with pitch. We bombed off a rope fixed to the overhanging branch of a river gum. We bombed till our guts ached. We caught leatherjackets and roasted their sweet flesh over a fire. We made damper out of flour and water, squeezed it around green sticks to cook over the coals. Once done, we'd pull the sticks out and pour golden syrup into the steaming holes.

Some days we'd row our loony canoes all the way to the lake, bailing water like crazy to keep afloat. We only came home when it grew dark, and only because we had to.

On other days we'd go further. We'd take our bikes and lay skid marks on all the gravel tracks to other lakes.

Some evenings, if the moon was high, we'd go prawning, the whole family. We'd drive to the lake at dusk and set up our lamps on the beach and light a fire under a large drum of salted water. We'd get the big dragnet out of the car and unfurl it on the beach. It had a long pole at either end with the net strung between them. We'd drag the net into the water with its long pocket trailing behind and trawl up and down a few times. Then we'd drag the net up the beach till the pocket was on the sand. There were always heaps of prawns and we'd throw them straight into the boiling water and eat them between thick buttered slices of white bread. All along the beach there were families prawning like us. Catching dinner on a school night!

Sometimes in early summer, when the big westerly winds drove the inland desert heat before them, when the air was so hot, it was hard to take a breath of it.

When the earth cracked and opened and the big gums sagged in the heat, a spark would strike and flare way back through the walls of bush, beyond the farmlands, deep in the backblocks.

Country people had the sense of it before they ever saw the smoke and long before the flames. It was the hint of a smell that sat on top of the breeze, rode it and made farmers lift from their work and stare.

There was nothing in our lives more threatening than a bushfire.

Nothing even came close.

The blue haze came first, and when it deepened the sun grew dim and red. We started the big diesel pump at the creek and wet the whole house down. We cleared the leaves from the gutters and filled the bath.

We waited.

When it came, the noise was deafening. It had its own internal wind that pushed it forward like a breath. The radiant heat was so intense the heads of the giant gums exploded, their burnt leaves showering down to ignite everything they touched.

Birds streaked across the sky, maddened by the heat. Wild things raced from the bush, burnt and blinded. Vast columns of acrid white smoke billowed a mile high, rising in heat-fuelled thermals to drift in the jet stream.

We stood blasted in a paddock of green and watched the demons dance before us. Great tongues of fire drove us back and back till all we could do was to cower and hope. We thrashed the edges of it with wet hessian bags for small victories. Finally, after it had left us, we trod through the X-rayed remnants of the bush, our footfall deadened by a layer of ash, the sour taste of smouldering charcoal on our tongues, to douse the spot fires that flared for days.

Death

There were other fires in other years. People died in them.

One family, new to the district, were overcome and incinerated in their new house. They were found all in one room in a charred huddle. The mother and baby had melted together to be forever as one. The father, at the top of the pyre, had tried to protect them all with a wide embrace that would last for eternity. We all went to look, to learn what sadness meant.

I had seen death before.

Once, on the school bus on our way home, we had slowed to a crawl to finally come upon the twisted crush of an accident on the highway.

The police and ambulance were there, and as we edged by we saw four bodies laid out on the grass verge under some yellow plastic. A light rain was falling on a pair of empty school shoes. A man wept in the arms of a policeman.

Death rode the highway. There were no seatbelts and no breath tests. You could drink till you were barely able to walk, but if you could make it to the car and actually get the thing started, you were free to go. Free, clear and deadly.

Aunty Vi, our other neighbour, had lost her husband three years before. There had been urgent voices at our door in the middle of the night. My father had gone with a lantern and sat with the stricken man while the life left him. Dad came home early the next morning, ashen-faced, and was quiet for a week. We saw the blackened polished car arrive that day and watched neat men carry Mr Tillock away forever.

A local farmer died when the tractor he was driving rolled over. I knew his son, Michael. His dad had ploughed all morning, and around midday had stopped for lunch. He had kicked off his muddy boots, gone into the house, sat down with his wife for a cuppa and a sandwich and probably a chat. An hour later he was back on the tractor when he hit a stump. He got off and tied the stout length of chain that he always carried with him around the stump, got back on, depressed the clutch with his left foot, engaged first gear and hit the gas. He started to release the clutch slowly to take up the strain, the stout chain snaking through the grass as the tractor inched forward. His foot slipped off the clutch because of the mud on his boots. The tractor shot forward, the chain whipped taut, the tractor reared, and the man saw an expanse of blue, blue sky before the machine crushed him and drove him deep.

Animals were different, they excused you from grief. There was always a valid reason for their deaths.

They made it easy for us to kill them.

I shot a blue wren with my slug gun, to see what would happen. I saw the exact moment when the life left it. But I was just a kid and it was just a bird.

It didn't pay to get attached to most of the animals at our place; you knew they weren't going to be around for long. The horses were safe but most everything else had a use-by date. The chooks were fairly temporary, which was a shame. I had names for all of them. There was Margaret, a big fat black chook. I named her after a big fat black chick I'd seen on TV. There was Carol, who was quiet and small and reminded me of a girl in my class.

Sometimes I'd put a washing-up glove on my head with all the finger bits sticking up. I'm pretty sure it made me look like a chicken. It mucked with the rooster's brain. He would watch me with a baleful eye, unsure of my intentions, his broad comb erect and the spurs on his legs trembling and ready.

Margaret was my favourite. I'd go down to collect the eggs and spend hours in the coop sitting in the straw. She would circle me slowly, chortling and clucking and raking through the hay for seeds and grit.

We killed our chooks and ate them. Sometimes at dinner, when Mum had put the roast chicken on the table, someone would say, 'Is this Margaret?'

I'd watch my father kill the chooks. We'd go into the chook pen and fight through the blur of feathers as they scattered, grab the chosen one by the legs and then carry it upside down to the chopping block and take its tiny head off with the axe. Sometimes they'd run around headless till their tiny hearts stopped and they lay still. We'd pluck the feathers and pull their guts out and they were ready to be eaten.

One time a local man brought a pig to our place. It stood in a sort of large pen on the back of this bloke's truck. He asked my father if he could kill and butcher it at our place, because he didn't have a shed of his own to hang it in. The old man agreed, for a share of the meat. I went to have a look at the pig. It was a whopper. Its little trotters seemed too small for it and its huge ears hung forward and covered most of its face. It seemed happy enough in its pen.

    I drifted over to where my father and the other bloke were discussing how best to dispatch the pig. It soon became clear that neither of them had the faintest idea as to how to go about it. There was mention of 'stunning' and the need to 'bleed' the meat, but the details were sketchy at best. After more discussion and head scratching it was decided by the quorum of two that they would lead the pig down to the paddock and, while one of them held the pig steady with a length of rope, the other would shoot it between the eyes. They would then transport it to the shed on the carryall that was attached to the tractor. There they would haul it up to the rafters and butcher the carcass. All good.

The old man goes to get his rifle, as he is the designated shooter. I wait with the other bloke as he coaxes the pig from the cage with the promise of an apple. The pig follows the bloke with the apple and with the help of a stout plank is soon off the back of the truck and, for the moment, safely on the ground. The old man returns with the loaded rifle and the pig obediently follows our solemn party down to the waiting paddock.

The pig gets another apple and the bloke with the rope turns the pig towards where my father is standing a few paces away. The bloke with the rope settles the pig. It's occupied with the last of the apple and seems happy enough. I retreat behind my father and look through the fingers of my hand in an attempt to lessen the horror of what I'm about to see. My father braces himself and lifts the rifle to his shoulder. The bloke with the rope retreats. The pig munches on the apple. Silence.

The rifle bucks. A puff of fine dust drifts from the pig's forehead. The pig munches on the apple. We wait …

The pig munches on.

The cows in the other paddock eat themselves forward.

A small plume of smoke curls from the hole in the forehead of the pig and mingles with the earlier dust to rise into the deathly quiet of the sky. No one moves. The rope lies slack in the pig bloke's hands. My father lowers the smoking gun. We wait, I watch, still squinting through the web of my fingers. The pig wonders why its ears are ringing, remembers the warmth of its mother and the taste of a sweet green apple and pitches forward on to the soft, tender grass.

They slit its throat then. The blood fairly gushes from the wound and empties the pig in a heartbeat. They string it up in the shed and shave the bristles short with the cut-throat razor, wash it down with boiling water, then set about it with the bright knives.

Another time Aunty Vi has a cow that has given birth. The calf is healthy, but the cow is showing signs of distress so the vet is called. My father goes to see if he can help, and I tag along.

We find the vet in the paddock with one arm up to the shoulder inside the cow. He says there's another calf inside, dead. This is too much for Dad, who flees the scene, both hands clutching his mouth.

I stay with the vet. He drops a metal ball deep into the cow. There is a fine wire attached to the end of the ball. He passes the ball around the body of the swelling calf and hauls the end of it from the rear of the cow. He holds the two ends of fine wire and starts to move them in a sawing motion. The idea is to cut the calf into pieces within the cow and remove the swollen body bit by bit. Now I understand why my father fled. The vet removes a leg sawn through the hip. He drops the steel ball back into the cow, retrieves the ends of fine wire and starts the sawing process again.

After fifteen long minutes, there is a jigsaw of body parts stacked in a bloody heap beside us, but the puzzle isn't yet halfway complete. The vet needs something from his van, so I take over. I feel the vibrations through the wire and the cut going deeper into the flesh and bone of the dead calf.

Finally the wire comes free as the vet arrives back and he plunges his arm deep inside the cow and retrieves the calf's head. The addition of the head starts to give the puzzle some meaning, but there's more to do.

We take a break to catch our breath. The living calf nuzzles its mother's udder and begins to feed. In the break the vet takes some blood from the cow and says that it has a massive infection and won't survive. He takes a lethal dose of barbiturate from his bag. I hold the cow's head and twist it to one side to expose a large vein in the neck. He plunges the needle into the vein and the cow dies on its feet and sags gently to the ground. The vet thanks me and goes to talk to Aunty Vi. I sit with the cow for a while till the warmth leaves her. I sit with the bits of a dead calf. I just sit.

Maybe it was a country thing, but we did see a lot of death.

I'm used to it, I can sit with it. I've seen the moment, the last thing.

We killed things; some for food, some, we thought, to protect us from being killed ourselves.

Like snakes!

We killed them all!

We had so many snakes around the farm that you'd hardly go a day without seeing one.

We had all the bad ones: red-bellied black, king brown – killers!

The worst time of year was early summer. They would come out of their long winter hibernation, the thick blood in them thinning now as the earth warmed, hungry and nasty. The marshy ground at the bottom of the farm was the perfect environment for them and they grew large and venomous.

My mother was hanging the clothes out one day in early December. The grass around the line was long and needed mowing. Mum had pegged a sheet on the line and was bending to pick up the next one when she saw the snake. It was a king brown, eight foot long and coming at her fast. She barely had time to lift the cane washing basket when it hit. The gaping mouth struck the basket and the venom flew from the front fangs. It came at her again and again, hissing and furious. She managed to keep it at bay till Dad arrived and took its head off with a spade. It squirmed for an hour till finally it lay still.

We used to throw the dead ones on the bull ants' nests. They'd be picked clean in a week.

I was getting my pushbike from the shed one day to ride to the lake. I heard a thumping sound from the roof above me. There, wrapped around one of the rafters, was a huge python. It must have been over ten foot long and as thick as my thigh. It had a fully grown possum locked between its jaws, and inch by agonising inch it was devouring it. I don't think I moved for an hour. I watched the possum disappear into the gullet of the snake as it squeezed and crushed it. Even after it disappeared I could still see the shape of the possum inching further through the length of the snake. We didn't kill pythons because they hunted the rats that plagued us, but that day I wished we did.

God, sport and rock'n'roll

I didn't think much about God at Lake Munmorah.

We lived so close to the land and our world was so small that we seemed closed off to anything else. Nobody I knew talked about God, certainly no one in my house.

My only contact with religion had been a brief stint at Sunday school, where the only thing we ever seemed to do was colour in pictures of Christ. I always gave Christ a bright red face; it seemed to suit him.

He always had his arms outstretched with his palms facing upwards.

He used to walk around all over the place with those arms outstretched and miraculously he didn't bump into many people. There he'd be in the middle of a crowd with people cowering all over the place, just trying to avoid those outstretched arms.

I think we were C of E.

I couldn't find anything to love about Christ.

I loved the Phantom, Mr Walker, the Ghost who Walks.

The Phantom kept things simple.

He loved a horse and a dog.

I think he also loved a girl called Diana, but only at the end of the comic, when things were getting a little slow.

Jesus, on the other hand, loved everybody, listened to everybody, created everything, and generally did too much to be believed. In the same way I had flicked the belief in Santa Claus when I was little, I had to let Jesus go too, because whether you flew around the world in one night delivering presents down a billion chimneys or you could turn water into wine but let four people die on the edge of a highway, in the end it just didn't wash. Too many inconsistencies. It only worked on little kids.

To me he was just a man with a red face.

*

My mate Sandy Dickie was religious. His family were Jehovah's Witnesses.

I had met some Jehovah's Witnesses before Sandy moved to the district.

Every now and then some Jehovah's or Seventh-Day Adventists would visit our farm to talk about God. I always thought that they were very brave, because nobody seemed to like them, but year after year they would come, their square worn shoes dusty from the miles of walking, smiling through our screen door as my family politely rejected them, again.

They truly believed in God. You could tell just by looking at them. They had a sort of light inside them that shone out. They would take the rejection that they must have known was coming, but you would never see it land on them and hold; they just carried on to the next farm to be turned away again.

Sandy had the same light in him. He never once talked to me about God, but sometimes he'd be gone for weeks with his family and I knew that he'd be walking some country road, smiling through other screen doors and telling people that God would save them.

He was a giant. He was twelve years old and well over six feet tall.

His religion would not allow him to play sport. We had started a rugby league team in the district and we wanted Sandy to be part of it. We were desperate to have him play, so we came up with a plan. We would turn up to his place on game day and ask his parents if he could come out to play with us. We would say we were going to the lake or to someone's house to do something or other. If we got the okay, we'd get Sandy to someone's house and get him dressed for the game. It was hard to get shorts to fit him and we couldn't find boots that came close. So we got some kid's father's work shorts and Sandy wore his own sandshoes, that looked bigger than the box they came in, and he was set to go.

He knew nothing about the game, but it didn't matter; he was a wrecking ball. We would just get the ball to him and watch. He would run the length of the field with half the other team on him, time and time again. Sometimes we'd give him a rest on the sidelines to give the other team a chance to score. We scored so many points in the first half of one game that the other team went home at half-time.

I was okay at footy – not spectacular, but steady, reliable. We called ourselves the Munmorah Red Devils, and played on a field our fathers had cut out of the scrub.

They had also built what was known as the Community Club on land provided by the council. The clubhouse was built right on the edge of the lake. It became a meeting place for the whole community. We used it for dances, wedding receptions, art shows, birthday parties, meetings, anything. One Saturday a month there would be a 50/50 dance at the clubhouse; 50/50 meant there would be a mix of old-time dances – like the Pride of Erin and the Progressive Barn Dance – and rock'n'roll. Everybody came, from little kids to grandparents. It was the only time when the whole community got together.

Between the dances women would gather in groups with little kids wound around their legs and chat over steaming cups of stewed tea.

Blokes hung out at the beer tent and lied to each other and laughed.

Bigger kids ran around the floodlit lawn at the front like dusty moths caught in the glare. Sometimes a fight would break out on the oval, at the edge of the light. The fighters, stripped to the waist, whaled into each other till exhaustion rather than injury halted the show and we all went in to dance again.

I loved the Progressive Barn Dance. Partner after partner coming at you, whirling and leaving, till a favourite arrived in a mist of perfume and heat that wrapped around you and stayed long after she'd gone.

Then the jittery rock'n'roll that made us all go wild with joy.

The Limbo Rock with the bar lowering and people clapping and urging you under, lower and lower till the last contorted body collapsed.

Later, chairs pulled together for sleeping kids. A bloke out the front with his head in hands moans, 'I think I've had enough. Here's the keys, love,' and spews. Cups and plates washed in lukewarm water from the last of the urn and racked to drain. Chairs, stacked in neat rows along a wall, while the brooms pushed the night back.

Cars spin in the dew on the oval and honk and weave into the night.

Later still the district sleeps and dreams of fingers interlaced and a broad hand in the middle of a backless dress, of the lucky punch, of a promise whispered for another night when he's at work and more – 'If you're good enough! Well, are ya?'

Diseases and maladies

You could get piles from sitting on cold concrete.

I never knew anyone with cancer.

Lots of old blokes died from heart attacks.

Most kids got measles, mumps and chicken pox and had their tonsils taken out.

Most baby boys were circumcised.

Some kids got whooping cough and had to go to hospital.

People didn't suffer from mental health problems. They seemed to just go mad suddenly. One day they'd be fine, the next they'd be eating pet food and licking their privates in the driveway. The big black van would arrive and they'd whack a straitjacket on them, take them to the nuthouse and hit them with a few volts to the brain. They'd be home in a fortnight and manageable for a week.

There seemed to be an awful lot of limping. People rocking themselves from here to there, swaying all over the place; maybe it was the polio.

A kid I knew got polio in the epidemic of 1956. He'd been taken to hospital with a severe burn on his leg from scalding water when he knocked the kettle off the stove at home. He contracted polio in hospital and ended up with a large boot on one foot and ugly callipers on his legs for life.

There weren't many spare parts around. So if you lost a bit of yourself, it pretty much stayed lost. You'd see the odd wooden leg. There'd be some poor bastard with his ruddy stump strapped to the top of one, clunking around the place. All that was missing was the parrot and the patch.

There were glass eyes. People who had them would just pop them out at night and put them in a glass beside the bed, next to the other glass that held their teeth. Next morning all they needed to do was give it a bit of a lick and pop it straight back in.

Most butchers only had four fingers. If you became an apprentice butcher, they'd cut one off for you, just to make you feel at home.

People never had epileptic fits at home. They'd wait till they were on a crowded bus or in a packed elevator before they'd let rip. I was on a bus in Newcastle when a woman had one. The conductor called for anyone with a pen or a pencil to stop her from swallowing her tongue. I lent him my new Staedtler HB with a rubber on the end that I'd only just bought. When I got it back it had teeth marks all over it and the rubber had been bitten off. I used to give kids a look at it for a bob.

Mum

Mum loved storms. She nearly called my sister Storm. Storm Bisley. It would have been different, that's for sure.

Anyway, Mum loved them.

The bigger the better, especially the summer ones.

They'd loom out of the south, usually in the afternoon of what had been a really hot day – what country folk called 'a stinker'.

She took me out once into a greying afternoon. A southerly had freshened and the temperature was dropping when a huge grey squall line unfurled above our house. The sky boiled and darkened. Great thunderheads formed on the southern horizon. Lightning spidered from the clouds, followed by a great whiplash crack of thunder, like something had broken. Then everything went still.

I wanted to race for the safety of the house but I stayed with her. Her face was turned upwards towards the turmoil above us. The lightning was jagged and as white as ice. The thunder started with a sound like splintering and then a great sonic boom that shook the house to the stumps.

She was smiling, even as the first drops splashed down. I stayed for as long as I could bear it and then ran to the shelter of the verandah. I watched her standing in the rain. Her feet were spread wide and her sodden dress clung to her like skin. She was a romantic, a dreamer and a poet, and she needed stuff with power and excitement in it. The storm did that for her. It fired her up. It invigorated her.

Mum kept people at arm's length. She'd lost faith in love, she'd been hurt and didn't want to be hurt again, so she closed her heart.

If you tried to get in there, to get close, she'd fold her arms so that her elbows pointed out like two blunt swords. You might get a pat on the head for comfort, but rarely anything else. Nothing close, that's for sure.

*

She was a career woman, which was unusual in the 1950s and early 1960s. Women were expected to keep a 'nice' home, look after their children and have a meal prepared when their husbands came home at night. Mum did all of that and more. By day she was a teacher at the local primary school. She was a born teacher. She captivated her students with her love of words and her ability to weave stories and fire their imaginations as she taught. At night, she'd make us dinner, help with homework and take care of all the small things that kids need.

Mum was the eldest of nine children. Her three sisters and five brothers were a handsome bunch.

The boys were all robust and the girls had an open beauty about them.

There were two framed photos in our house. One was of my mother as a young woman. She looks like a 1940s movie star, radiant and assured. The other was of my father in his Air Force uniform with a blue military cap placed jauntily on his head. His face had been coloured. There was a blush on his cheeks and his lips were redder than in life. It was a handsome face, and smooth. I could see why they would have been attracted to each other.

After they were married and the war had ended, they, like many thousands of survivors of the war, took their hopes, dreams and fears and scattered them across new horizons.

I don't know when my father stopped loving Mum and started to love anyone.

I don't know if he ever loved her at all.

I don't think he knew what love was.

Dad

I was born into a world of Men.

Of Warriors.

They strode back from the war, the hot yeast rising in their young veins.

Victorious.

'Look what we have done,' was their battle cry. 'We have saved you!'

The question was, who would save us from them?

After their battalions were disbanded they found themselves discharged, unwanted, alone.

All these damaged men.

I knew my father had enlisted in the Air Force in the Signal Corps and had served in New Guinea. He was twenty-one years old. That was all I knew. He never spoke of the war or his part in it. The subject was off limits, taboo. So he sat with it by himself for years and let it seep into him. He owned it and nobody was going to take it from him, and every Anzac Day he marched with all these other men to remember something they were all desperately trying to forget.

We had books about the war at home and I read them carefully in an attempt to find out what it must have been like for Dad.

New Guinea! Kokoda! The humid wetness of the place. They'd gone to that strange foreign land from the dust and heat of home where rain was a blessing, not a curse. To rain that shredded the coconut palms and bogged the camps with mud to the knees. A scratch became a wound in a day in the seeping wet, and 'dry' was a memory. Malaria and dysentery plagued them. Their feet rotted in their boots. The dense tracts of jungle encircled them on all sides. They were vastly outnumbered by the Japanese as the main body of the Australian defence force was fighting another enemy on the battlefields of Europe. The Japanese Army had a policy of not taking prisoners in New Guinea and there were stories of captured Australian soldiers being tied to trees in the jungle and used for bayonet practice. Beheading was another favourite tactic employed by the enemy.

I don't know what my father was like before the war.

I only know what he was like after.

Damaged.

I don't know what my father endured over there. What he saw, what he did, what he had done to him. I could only imagine.

Lest We Forget. There was no chance of that.

The grans and nans

My father's mother is coming to live with us today!

We didn't discard our old people; we kept them like worn shoes.

She's going to live in my room till she dies!

So I've got to bunk in with my sister in doll land. Great.

Nan's got dementia, which means she thinks she's a chicken. Maybe I can put a washing-up glove on her head and she can come down to the chook shed and sit with me and Margaret. She doesn't think she's a chicken all the time, though; she thinks she's lots of things. She's not nuts, just confused. Maybe I should scatter a little cracked wheat around my old room before she arrives, just to make her feel at home.

I move the last of my *Phantom* comics and stack them beside the doll's house in my sister's room. I leave my six-gun and a roll of caps in my bedside drawer just so Nan doesn't forget the sacrifice I've made for her.

Like with all my father's relatives, I've hardly ever seen Nan. All I really know about her is that she's old.

We drive to Sydney to pick her up from her house in Manly, not far from the Corso, with its face to the west and its back to the sea. There's only Mum and Dad and me, so there'll be room for Nan on the way home. The house is dark brick and squat. A nurse meets us at the door. We go in. Nan's in the kitchen pouring freshly brewed tea into a pot plant. The nurse rescues the pot and the tea gets poured into the waiting cups. Nan chortles happily and calls me Roger. She thinks Dad is a doctor and wonders who Mum is. I leave the confusion in the kitchen and go for a wander.

There are two ancient Easter eggs in a locked glass cabinet in the living room. Each egg is in the centre of a dusty glass shelf, like forlorn trophies from another time. They had always tempted me on our rare trips to Sydney when I was little. I'd stand close to the dark cabinet, forbidden to touch it, but longing for a taste of them, to feel the chocolate soften and melt and slide on my tongue. The weevils had found them years ago. Their lacy trails crisscrossed each decaying egg to leave them powdered beneath the ageing foil. Everything in decay and dying here.

A piano with yellowing ivory keys.

Tattered velvet curtains dim the daylight to shadows.

Pine cones in a cold fireplace.

Brass candlesticks in shapes of rearing cobras hold the forgotten nubs of candles.

Sepia faces in dark frames stare blankly into the gloom.

Thinly papered walls faded and fading.

My long-dead grandfather haunts me from another lifeless frame. The chain from his fob watch loops into the pocket of a dark vest. Pince-nez glint from the bridge of his aquiline nose. I fart loudly to see if my grandfather's expression changes. It doesn't. I fart again, just for fun.

Why do all sepia photographs appear so sad, dull and lifeless? What happened to the fun?

There's another tortured photo beside my grandfather's. It's my father as a child. He has the same sullen look as his own father. Just a sad little boy in a bad suit. No wonder my grandmother can't remember anything. Who'd want to?

I go further into the house in search of the love, of something soft, a hint of something from the heart. There is the smell of old in every room, like watery cabbage. A bedroom. Cut crystal jars on the dressing table, wispy hairs trail from a silver brush, an ivory-topped cane leans against a dark-panelled dresser.

In my grandfather's study, solemn books, grim and heavy, line the walls. *Ode to a Country Churchyard* and more odes and weary sonnets. This whole place, a shrine to the miserable. A roll-top desk darkens a quiet corner. He's been gone for years but it feels like he's never left. His cold pipe lies half packed beside his heavy leather armchair. Did he ever run around naked in the house with Christmas tinsel tied around his balls? Did he and my grandmother lie naked in bed on a Sunday, send my dad to the pictures and fuck till lunchtime? Did he ever cuddle my father and wrestle him to the floor and tickle him till he wet his pants? Did he build things with him, have adventures, tell him about girls, kiss him and tell him that he loved him so much it hurt? A pig flies past the window.

I slope back to the joys of the kitchen.

Four things in the pantry, three things in the fridge. Nan asleep in a chair as the others busy themselves around her. Her life in a small suitcase. I escape the house for light and air.

Dad's coming now and Nan's inching along on two canes past the For Sale sign to the waiting car. St Vinnies are coming tomorrow to empty her life into boxes and sell them, cut price, to strangers. Mum folds Nan neatly into the back seat. I slide in beside her.

'Do you know my father?' she asks.

'No, Nan,' I reply.

'He was very difficult at times.'

We turn out of Nan's street for the last time.

I know what she means.

It's going around.

I got my room back after only a few months. Nan's confusion grew to the point where it just became too hard to manage and she had to go into care.

It was such a shame.

I really miss the eggs.

My mother's mum was a different kettle of fish altogether. Jessica, my maternal grandmother, had been a 'tweeny', a between-stairs maid, in a large house in Shepherd's Bush in London in the early 1900s. She had worked upstairs in the main living area of the house, serving at table, making beds and cleaning, as well as downstairs in the kitchen as needed.

She met my grandfather, who was the local coal man, at the back door of the big house. They fell in love and soon after immigrated to Australia, Jessie pregnant with my mother. Jessie told stories of the First World War and had sharp recollections of the bombing of London, of food rationing and small coffins being taken away from her parents' house after several of her siblings had died of illnesses like diphtheria and influenza. She had a rich cockney accent and a mad sense of humour. She drank a single glass of OP rum diluted with a little water every day.

Some of my mother's brothers and sisters built their houses on vacant land right next to Gran's, just to be near her. She was the centre of all our lives and, although we lived a long way from Sydney, we always knew Gran was there for each and every one of us.

Visitors

I'm swinging on the big wire gate at the entrance to our farm. I open the gate as far as it will go. I take a few paces back and run like mad and jump on. This sends the gate hurtling towards the big fence post. If you're not holding on really tightly, it will buck you off when it smashes into the post.

This is what I do when I'm waiting for visitors to arrive.

My cousin Wocky is coming up from Sydney with his parents and I hope he gets here soon 'cause my hands have blisters on them now from swinging on this bloody gate. Usually I only swear when I'm by myself. It's safer that way. Sometimes I say 'shit' and 'bloody' together, like this: 'Shit, I think I'll have another ride on this bloody gate while I'm waiting for my bloody cousin to arrive!'

I swear at Dukey the dog all the time, and I can tell he really likes it. 'Come here, you pooftah,' I say and he wags his tail like mad. He doesn't know what it means and neither do I but it sounds great.

All swear words sound great!

Fuck sounds the best.

Do you want to know what happened when I first said it?

We were having dinner and I said to my brother, 'Pass the fucking butter, please.' My friend Wayney Brooks had told me at school that day that you could say 'fuck' if you were asking for something. Sounded pretty good to me so that's why I gave it a go.

Things got really quiet, really quickly. Richard nearly choked on a mouthful of food; he went bright red and wouldn't look up from his plate. Kris dropped her knife and fork with a clatter, Mum put her hand to her mouth and it seemed like she was laughing behind it and Dad looked like he'd seen a ghost.

After things settled down and were back to normal it was my mother who remained at the table after everyone had hurriedly left. When she had composed herself, Mum warned me that if she heard me use that word again she would wash my mouth out with soap.

Fuck! I thought. Fuck!

I hear the sound of a car coming; it has to be them 'cause hardly anyone ever comes down our road. My brother says that the reason nobody comes is because we live in the arsehole of the world. There's another beauty!

I have a final swing on the fucking arsehole of a gate, crashing into the post as their car comes into view. 'Visitors!' I yell towards the house, and by the time they're through the gate we're all there to meet them.

The parents all head into the house for tea, but I've got something special to show Wocky because he's from the city and doesn't know much about the bush.

I take him around the shed and through the gate to the paddocks below.

We have three horses: Tiger, a piebald stallion; Bootsy, a short fat pony; and Honey, our brood mare. We ride them all, but Honey doesn't like to be ridden and always tries to bite you on the fucking arse when you're least expecting it.

Today, though, Honey is going to have a foal. We always know when a foal is going to be born because Tiger gets really excited and charges around the paddock like a mad thing. He's been doing it all morning.

I tell Wocky all this as we climb to the top rail of the fence. Honey is standing really still. She's not very far away from us. Her body is stiff and her back legs are trembling. I call her but she doesn't come. I know what's about to happen, I've seen it before, but Wocky is in for a surprise.

Tiger rears high on his back legs and races the length of the paddock, bucking and twisting. Honey stands steady, unmoving. Her back legs are bending now and the muscles through her sides are rippling with the contractions. Sweat glistens on her flanks. Suddenly blood gushes from her rear and a small head appears, and in an instant the foal falls gently to the soft clover, wet from the birth.

Bang!

Wocky's head moves sideways about a foot when the blow hits him. It's his father! He hauls Wocky from the fence and tells him it's disgraceful that he's been watching and he's to go and wait in the house till they're ready to leave. Then he turns on me – I should be ashamed that I let Warren see something like that, he says.

I don't understand. Getting a flogging for watching a foal being born? I wait on the fence, alone. I look at the new foal lying wet in the grass and Honey nuzzling her gently and I'm glad I live here, on my farm in the bush.

I'd rather a paddock full of horses than a room full of people any fucking day.

Scissors

We never see it coming, never, until it's too late.

I'm in the willow tree with Kris. It's in a corner of our yard, not far from the house but far enough for secrets. It's Kris's favourite tree. We've built cubbies all through the bush, but right here is her special place.

I know why she likes it. There is a softness to this tree, a gentleness that she needs. Its branches are smooth and its leaves cascade in a light green shower that trails the ground.

On other days she's good in a tree. She moves easily and hugs the main trunk as she climbs. Today is different, and wrong. She's carrying a pair of long scissors tucked into the waistband of her shorts.

She wants to climb to the very top of her favourite tree and fall to the ground so that the scissors will split her guts open and she will die.

I wonder what her guts will look like after the fall. Will the scissors still be sticking out or will they be pushed right inside her guts from the impact? The willow shudders as she nears the top.

I wonder if she will die right away or if she will be talking to me for a while before she dies. I wait in the lower branches and think about life without her.

I know why she's up there.

We both got a belting an hour ago.

We'd been fighting instead of doing a job we'd been given.

Push-and-shove stuff, it's never serious.

We were told to each go and pick a stick from the bush and take it to the shed and wait.

Always the waiting. Waiting for what is coming, hoping for the reprieve that never comes. We are both in the cool dimness of the shed, not looking at each other now, waiting, caught.

Waiting for the sound of his feet on the gravel outside. His shoes shifting the sharp stones as he walks towards us. But not till the waiting is done, till it's been enough time, does he come.

My eyes dart around the shed.

My heart is loud in my ears.

There is nothing soft in here.

Hard things line the walls.

Crowbars, pickaxes, loops of wire, hammers, saws with razor-sharp teeth, pliers. On the workbench are two vices with their jaws cranked wide open.

Light from empty nail holes in the roof cut the gloom in shafts. My sister's eyes never leave the floor, but her body twists in defiance. She knows she is now too old for this, too smart. She knows that what is coming won't make her understand anything she doesn't already know.

Our sticks of choice are in our hands.

We have chosen carefully.

Too thin means they'll break too early and the fury will continue with a belt or worse.

Too thick and the welts will be raw and deep.

There is a crunch outside and then another, measured and quickening.

My eyes go to my sister; her legs are buckling in preparation for the blows, her stout stick is quivering in her hand.

Then he is at the door.

Then inside with us.

His face is ruddy, white spittle blisters his lips and he is shaking and furious. He wrenches the stick from my sister's hand and cuts a great whistling arc with it. Again and again the stick flails against her till she is screaming and pleading. 'I'll be good, Dad!' she cries, and, 'No, Dad, no! Please, no!'

Now his rhythm is set and the blows come harder and harder till I'm crying for her and yelling too. 'Please stop, Dad! No, Dad, please – it's my fault!'

Our voices mix and the blows come faster and the spittle flies and he flings the first stick away and now he's into me. The stick breaks and he is punching me with his fists and now he pulls a handful of hair from my head as a fist splits my bottom lip open. I see Kris on the floor, great welts on the backs of her legs, and her face is set like something wild.

Then Mum is there in the doorway, screaming, 'Stop, Bruce, stop! Please God, stop!'

Then he is gone.

And he has broken us.

Again.

We sit in the willow till the dark comes.

Shops

There was a post office run by Mr and Mrs O'Connor. They were as old as dirt. They had the grey skin that only old people had. Grey skin with blotchy brown liver spots everywhere. Long saggy faces with glasses perched on the end of their noses. They had old mangy dogs that stunk. There was no mail delivery so people had to collect their letters from the post office. Nobody stayed to chat because of those stinking dogs. The smell of the dogs was on everything. On the front counter were tall glass jars with lollies in them, and if you were crazy enough to buy any, then one of the old O'Connors would thrust a dog-smelly hand into the jar and claw out your selection. It just wasn't worth it.

The post office was also the telephone exchange. Our telephone number was Lake Munmorah 2. To make a telephone call you turned a handle on a box that was attached to the telephone. This caused a bell to ring at the post office. One of the old O'Connors would plug a cord into a hole and say, 'Hello?' You would then ask for the number you wanted. If I wanted to call my cousin I would ask for Lake Munmorah 4. They would then plug a cord into a hole marked 4 and turn another handle and my cousin's phone would ring. When you had finished your call you would say goodbye to the O'Connors because they were always listening in.

If you wanted to call a number in Sydney it could take up to an hour to connect.

There were no shops, so things got delivered. There was the Watkins man. He came in a large van. It was stocked with all the things that women needed to run a lovely house. There was hand soap for the bathroom and laundry soap that was chunky and yellow and harsh. There was Solvol, a grey, gritty soap used for getting stubborn stains out of anything. There were blue bags – small muslin bags with strong blue detergent inside that women would use in the copper. The copper was a large round container set inside a brickwork outer casing with a firebox underneath. The copper was filled with water and the fire beneath was lit, causing the water inside to boil furiously. The blue bag was cast into the boiling water and the clothes were then added and the whole thing was stirred with a large bleached stick. After the clothes had been exposed to this treatment for sufficient time they were hauled out and put through a medieval device aptly named 'the mangle', which squeezed every last drop of water from them. This procedure was used for whites and bed linen and the like, and I have never lain on sheets that were cleaner than those that had been put through the copper-and-mangle routine.

The Watkins man also sold towels, sheets, tea towels and cutlery. He wore a grey dustcoat and his hair was greased back with fine comb lines running through it from front to back. I always thought the Watkins man was a bit suss, and stayed close to Mum when he called, because my brother told me the Watkins man was always 'givin' women one' behind his van. I didn't know what that meant, but I didn't want it to happen to Mum.

*

I used to hang out for the baker to arrive. He was my favourite visitor.

He came once a week and would open a flap on the side of his truck and prop it up with a stick he carried. Inside were shelves lined with all sorts of bread and cakes. Cream horns, apple turnovers, horseshoes, vanilla slices, lamingtons, apple pies, custard tarts and the smell of warm bread. Sometimes he'd give us kids a loaf for nix and we'd pull out the doughy centre and fill the hole with butter and Vegemite.

The Carters' big house

Janice and Helen!

The Carter girls next door had a real cubby house. Not like the ones that we threw together in the bush; a couple of rough poles leant against a tree covered in leafy branches. Theirs was a real one. It had fibro walls, with sliding windows and a real door. It had an iron roof with a pretend chimney on it. It was painted in girly colours, like pink and green. Inside was a kitchen with a stove that didn't work and a wooden fridge.

Best of all there were two bunks, real beds you could sleep in or just lie on, mucking around. We used to play all sorts of games in the cubby. When we were young, it was just pots and pans, and making cakes out of sand and water, and dressing up in adult clothes and pretending to be Mum or Dad.

Later we'd play Spin the Bottle, and you'd have to kiss whoever it landed on. I loved kissing and used to practise with my cousin Linda, who lived across the creek.

Sometimes I'd have to be the doctor and Janice and Helen would be the patients. I'd knock on the door and someone would call, 'Come in.'

There'd be giggling from the bunks. I'd go in with my bag of stick-like instruments. The treatment was always the same and usually had something to do with their panties.

The Carters had the first TV in the area because they were rich. Everyone in the district was invited to come and watch *Bonanza* on Friday night. People came from everywhere, swinging their lanterns along bush tracks to see the wonder of this thing called TV. It was black and white and beautiful. It was like having the movies in your house whenever you wanted to watch them. It was like a genie had come out of a box. The magic of television held us from the first moment we saw it, and it would never let us go.

So there we'd be, a dozen kids on the carpet with the adults behind us on chairs with cups of tea, watching our future in black and white. Later they got a special bit of plastic that you stuck to the front of the TV. It was meant to turn a black and white picture into colour. The top of the plastic was blue, for the sky. The middle bit was pink, for skin tones. The bottom strip was green to match the colour of grass. Yep, that was the first colour TV. It sort of worked, if the picture on the screen was of someone standing outside on the grass under the sky, but mostly it was just plain weird.

We still didn't have the power on.

We had a radio, powered by big Eveready batteries covered in a sort of waxy paper to stop the acid leaking out of them. Every evening at five o'clock, no matter where you were, you'd belt home in time for *The Children's Hour* on the ABC. You could become an Argonaut, sailing the seas in search of the Golden Fleece. As an Argonaut you were given your own special number and, if you wrote into the show and answered a quiz question correctly, they would read out your name and number for everyone who was listening to hear.

There were also serials. There was *Randy Stone*, an American reporter who covered the night beat for a daily newspaper. He got into all sorts of trouble with gangsters and lowlife people and girls who spelt trouble with a capital T.

There was *Reach For the Sky*, the story of Ol' Tin Legs, Douglas Bader, who had lost his legs in a plane crash. With courage, determination and a pair of metal legs, he became a World War II flying ace!

There were quiz shows and loads of music. The radio fuelled your imagination because you made the pictures in your head. You knew what the blonde that Randy had just rescued looked like. You were in the plane with Ol' Tin Legs, in the heat of battle; you could smell the smoke from the engine of his burning plane as he plummeted to earth.

If Dad came home with fish and chips on a Friday night, we knew we were going to the drive-in. We'd have our dinner straight out of the paper parcel. Steamy potato chips and battered fish with vinegar and lemon squeezed over. Then we'd all get in the Jag for the ride to Newcastle.

When we got there the light would be fading and we'd park our car with its nose tilted up towards the big screen. Dad unhooked the small speaker from its pole and sat it on the dashboard. Tinny music filled the car. It was so exciting!

Gradually night fell and the big screen lit up. There was always a cartoon before the film started, sometimes *Bugs Bunny* or *Daffy Duck*. We'd snuggle up under a blanket in the back seat, each with our own pillow, and watch. I don't think I ever saw the end of a film, I always nodded off, but what I did see was pure magic.

The West

There is a huge, black steam locomotive waiting at a platform at Central Station in Sydney. Great clouds hiss from the lungs of the boiler. Men in faded bib-and-brace overalls feed the glowing firebox with square-mouthed shovelfuls of flinty black coal. Relief valves fizz with jets of steam. Mum and us kids are going on a holiday to our cousins' farm. They live in Gilgandra, near Dubbo, in the west of New South Wales. It's not even school holiday time, but some things happened between my parents.

Dad drove us to Sydney, but he's not coming with us. He's staying home to mind the farm and do what men do when they want to be alone. Or when they want to be with someone else. Dad wrestles our luggage from the car. We stand with our mother. Dad tells us to be good.

'Yes, Dad,' we chorus. We watch the Jaguar slice into the city traffic. I slide my hand into Mum's as we watch him go.

We find our carriage and haul our luggage down the narrow passageway to our compartment. It's a sleeper. There are two long padded seats that face each other and a silver wash basin set into shiny wood panelling. By night the seats become bunks, with two more that fold out from the walls. Above the bunks are stout wire racks for our luggage.

There is a picture of a train crossing a bridge over a river. I love our compartment. It's like a cubby house, with all of us snug and close.

We unpack our books, comics and coloured pencils for later, and while Mum and Kris settle in, Rich and I head off to explore the train. We jump out onto the platform for another look at the loco. There's a swarm of blokes all over it and it stinks of coal smoke. There are other boys watching too, all of us drawn by the power of it. One bloke, big and sweaty from the heat, grins at us and yanks on a greasy rope above his head. Jets of steam screech from the big silver whistle above. 'Youse better git on – we're leavin'!'

We streak back down the platform and leap onto the train as the guard yells, 'All aboard!' Two more blasts on the whistle and the big steel couplings take up the strain as the wheels spin and grip the rails. We lurch out of the station with me and Rich careering to our compartment.

I am so excited! Mum tells me to settle down, we've got a long way to go, but I can't help myself. I'm on a holiday, on a train, in a sleeper, and I've got a new *Phantom* comic! And Dad's not here! Who wouldn't be excited?

Rich plonks down in the seat opposite me and gives me the finger. I laugh like crazy, 'cause he's so stupid. My sister asks Mum to tell us to stop, but I want him to keep going forever, 'cause he's just the best at anything in the world.

We head west through the sprawl of the suburbs and climb the steep Blue Mountains to clatter down onto the Western Plains. We play Fish with cards and Pick-Up Sticks and I Spy. We eat the curling corned-beef sandwiches and drink stewed tea from the thermos. We range along the snaking length of the train in search of other kids to tease and chase. I read the *Phantom* comic twice and wrestle with Rich till I say Uncle as he twists my ear. I snooze a bit and wake in fields of wheat in the late afternoon.

Later we go to the dining car and I get a mixed grill for tea and apple pie for afters. It's all so special, me and my family having tea on a train. I think of Dukey the dog at home with Dad. Dad alone in his place at the head of the table with a frothy beer and his lonely dinner. I know that if he wanted to he could be here with us. He never wants to.

When we get back to our sleeper, the beds have been made with crisp white sheets and snuggly blankets folded back. Mum and Kris go to the ladies' to change for bed, while Rich and me find our flattened PJs in our bag. He tells me to take the bottom bunk because he thinks if I have the top one I could fall out in the night and smash my skull open and my brains would fall out and I would die. I half believe him and crawl into the bunk below him for a last look at the *Phantom*. I flick my reading light on and open the comic. Someone has drawn a penis in pencil sticking out of the Phantom's head and another one on his horse.

I want to get really upset but I am laughing too much. I kick my blankets off and shove my feet against my brother's mattress above and push like mad. He's bouncing like crazy and says if I don't stop he will punch my lights out. Mum returns and we fall quiet. I snuggle down in my bed to the swaying of the carriage as the big loco hauls us deeper into the night. Later I wake briefly to the sound of my mother crying softly in the dark.

Next morning the train pulls into Dubbo. Uncle Les is there with his broad country hat and his too-pale skin. He calls Mum 'Paulie' and kisses and hugs her warmly. We head to the car to drive the forty-odd miles to Gilgandra and the farm. The country feels enormous out here; there is barely a tree for miles and the sky is huge and cloudless. Flocks of sulphur-crested cockatoos wheel above us in their hundreds. Dead kangaroos litter the roads and emus race along the fence lines. Fields of wheat stretch to the horizon.

We arrive at the homestead in a cloud of red dust. I'm barely out of the car and suddenly shy when my cousin Paul, who's the same age as me, claims me in a bear hug and wrestles me to the ground with his maniacal grin and freckled face pushed into mine. 'G'day, cuz!' he screams.

'Been waitin' for weeks fur you to git here! Got something to show ya!' With that, he hauls me to my feet and drags me full pelt into the house.

'Check this out!' We are standing in front of a large gun rack in the hallway. Six rifles are arranged in a neat row. He hauls the lowest one down and slides the bolt up and back then slams it back into the breech. 'The old man bought it for me a week ago. I haven't put one through it yet but we're going after roos tonight, spotlightin'. You can use me old one – here!' He reaches for the next rifle on the rack and thrusts it at me. He grabs a box of bullets from a cupboard and then we're heading out the door. 'Dad? I'm taking Stevie down the gorge to shoot some cans. Be back in an hour.' I hear Mum protest but Uncle Les quietens her and we're free to go.

Paul leads me to an enormous shed full of vehicles of all sorts. There are tractors and motorbikes, trucks in various sizes, several utes and a Land Rover with the roof cut off. He jumps into the Land Rover, reaches over and wrenches the other door open. 'Git in, ya big sheila,' he says, and fires up the motor. I'm barely in my seat when we swerve out the door and he points the Rover up a flinty track beside the sheep yards. Here we are, going flat strap in a car driven by an eleven-year-old, with two rifles and enough ammo to start a small war. It was only a few hours ago that I was worried about somebody drawing a penis on the Phantom's head. We crest the hill behind the homestead going full stick and I can't stop the grin that's plastered on my face. It's probably a mix of adrenalin and joy with a pinch of the fear of death; whatever it is, I never want it to stop.

We come to a screeching halt above a gully where deep ruts of erosion cut the clayey soil to the bedrock.

Rusted car bodies litter the gully floor with bits of machinery, old bedframes, buggered mattresses, offcuts of wood, broken crockery, fruit boxes and a porcelain dunny. Crows pick through rotting food and hang like black rags above the dumped things.

We climb out of the Rover. Paul pulls the bolt back to expose the breech and drops the empty magazine into his hand, and by the time we have perched on the rim of the gorge he has slid a handful of bullets into the clip and worked the bolt to spear a round into the breech.

'Gunna shoot with a scope tonight but for now I've just got to shoot it in. Let's see how she goes.' He passes me the box of bullets and brings the rifle up to press against the side of his cheek. 'See that fuckin' dead crow?'

'Which one?' I ask.

The gun bucks in his hands and one of the hovering black rags falls through its own red mist and feathers to the flinty ground. 'That one!' he leers. The sound of the gunshot spirals around the gorge. 'Not too bad, just has to come up a bit,' and he turns a knurled adjuster on the rear sights.

I'm still feeding bullets into my magazine when the second shot roars and misses.

'Shit,' says Paul and fingers the adjuster again.

I bring the rifle to my shoulder. I've shot before and know the deal. I avoid the crows and draw on an old chrome mirror on a rusted car door. I pull the rifle stock into my shoulder and brace for the recoil. I take a slow breath and hold it like I've been taught while the crook of my finger tightens lightly on the black curve of the trigger. The V on the rear sights finds the tiny pyramid of steel on the front of the barrel; my finger squeezes. The rifle bucks and the mirror explodes in a shower of bright shards.

'Fuck the car parts!' says Paul. 'Get into the crows. We hate 'em out here 'cause they pick the eyes outta the lambs.'

I slide the bolt back and the shiny casing of the spent bullet spins into the dirt and the next one slides home into the breech. I feel the warmth of the wooden stock against my cheek as I breathe and hold again and find a crow in the sights. I track it as I pull the stock further into my shoulder and before I squeeze I let the gun drift till all I see through the sights is the colour blue. The gun bucks and the crow flies on. 'Damn,' I pretend.

We head back to the homestead. I get a big hug from Aunty Eileen and my cousin Robyn, who kisses me on the mouth and lingers too long. Kris is sharing a bedroom with her and Rich is with my cousin John. Mum looks really pleased to see me and gives me a rare hug.

It's about the gun.

*

We all have dinner around the big table in the kitchen. It's dark by the time Uncle Les leads us back to the big machinery shed. Just us, the blokes.

We all carry rifles, barrels pointed down for safety, the breeches gaping open and empty. There are others waiting in the shadows, professional shooters. No-fuss, no-mucking-around blokes. Two fresh carcasses swing from a rack in the back of a ute.

'Bowled these two on the way over, Les. There's a shitload down by the dam.'

We head out in a loose convoy. Uncle Les drives the flatbed truck with me, Paul, Richard and Johnny on the back. There is a padded bar that runs across the cab of the truck to rest the rifles on. I am in the centre with Paul, the bigger boys at either end. We track the fence line. The moon is high and bright now as we hit the downgrade. The dam below us shimmers. A night breeze rustles the wheat. The engines quiet as we roll forward. Everything stills. There is just the sound of the rifles being loaded and the roos feeding in the dark.

I feel the wild adrenalin in my chest as I lift the gun. The spotlights flare and shock the night awake. The roos are caught and blinded, helpless in the ravaged wheat. Gunfire cracking from all sides. Bodies twisting and falling from the head shots; a joey flung from his mother's pouch stands helpless in the glare. The rank smell of cordite drifts in the night. A big red, wounded, escapes the blinding light and lurches awkwardly towards the boundary fence, the once powerful back legs weakened from the blood loss. He leaps, but is caught by the barbed wire and hangs there like a torn coat. They shoot him where he hangs and leave him for the wild dogs to claim.

Then stillness again as the wounded are quietened by bright knives and loaded onto the flatbed. We drive to other paddocks and shoot and shoot till the racks on the ute are full and the flatbed springs groan under the weight of the dead ones. I don't know whether I've killed or wounded anything. I shot at things, I know that, so I own the killing like the rest and I feel bigger with the gun in my hands.

After, we drive home under a waning moon. I watch the hunters tear the skin from the shiny bodies and butcher them down to neat parcels. They salt the skins and hang them high for curing. We wash the blood down from the trucks and empty and oil the rifles.

It's midnight when Paul and I head to our beds in the sleepout. We talk in the dark for a while. He tells me he has seen his sister's pubic hair through a hole in the bathroom wall and, if I want him to, he will show me tomorrow. I tell him it's okay 'cause I've seen plenty of pubic hair and, anyway, I know where my father hides his condoms. I slide lower into the strange bed. Paul's gone suddenly quiet and I know I've got him with the condom line.

I wait in the now quiet room till I hear his breathing settle and I know he is sleeping. I creep from my bed and find my way through the darkened house to Mum's room. She knows it's me and calls my name softly in the night. I nestle in beside her, just me and Mum.

We stayed at our cousins' farm for the next two weeks. The shearers came to shear the mobs of squat merinos. Lanky blokes in dusty utes threw their swags on rusty beds in the shearers' quarters. They rolled skinny fags as they thought of things to say, and then thought better of it and didn't speak. They stuck pictures of their kids and dogs and the missus above their beds, to ease the nights. They had their own way of standing, with one hip kicked out and the weight of them going back to leave the front leg resting and their boots drawing shapes in the dust. They never looked at you when they spoke and their words slid out sidewards and there weren't many of them.

We sat at an open fire with them one night after tea, us kids. The fire caught us all and held us. They passed bottles of dark rum between them and told stories of other sheds. Of blokes not worth working for and other blokes who were, of a record set in a southern shed but that was with a wide-toothed comb on the shears so it wasn't really legal, but either way, who's counting. A tinny radio played country music and a girl sang about her truck-driving man and a screen door hittin' somebody in the arse on the way out. I'd love to hit somebody in the arse with a screen door! They didn't pay much attention to us, but I loved being around the quiet ease of them. We all did, you could feel it.

We'd go down and watch them at work through the day.

The sheds were buzzing in the heat.

The smell of lanolin from the fleece.

There was a row of nine of them, all bent at the waist, the clippers whirring in their hands. The brown kelpies worked the holding pens and drove the unshorn ones up the races to the waiting blades. Minutes later the sheep would leave the sheds naked and white without the wool. The fleece was then thrown across the classing table, checked for quality and stacked for cleaning. Sweat traced the muscle down a sinewed arm.

Smoko!

The big diesel quiet. Black tea out of a chipped enamel mug. A cheese and pickle sandwich and half a fag. Cicadas droning in the big river gums. The shed shimmering in the heat.

Then the diesel fires up and it's on again till dusk.

On other days we swam in the dam where the water tasted like dirt.

A foot below the surface it reddened and further down it went dark and cold. We covered ourselves in the red mud and slid down the banks to wash it from our slippery skins.

We drove for miles out to the front gate to check the mail and no one worried that we were kids. We rode horses and raced each other flat-out.

Some nights Uncle Les would set up a movie projector and we'd watch cartoons against the lounge-room wall. Or we'd have a concert. I tried to perform the song about the screen door hitting someone in the arse on the way out, but I couldn't remember the words.

We had such fun!

Finally it was the night before we had to leave. Paul told me to be really quiet and he led me in the dark to the outside of the bathroom wall. As we got closer I could hear the sound of the shower inside. Paul put his finger to his lips and quietly removed a large nail and pointed to the hole. I pressed my eye to it. There in the glow of the light was my cousin Robyn. She was naked, and although I wanted to run from the shock of it, something held me firm to the wall and I knew in an instant that my life had changed – forever.

They all come to the station to see us off the next morning. Aunty Eileen has made us sandwiches and cakes for the trip and Uncle Les shakes my hand and says he'll make a shearer out of me yet. Paul gets me in a farewell headlock and says he's gunna miss me like shit and I believe him. I say goodbye to Johnny. I can't look at Robyn 'cause my face gets hot and something happens in my pants. But she doesn't know and kisses my lips, which makes everything worse, and I bolt onto the train.

We find our compartment as the train leaves and settle in for the trip home. Later, as we all lay in our bunks, I watch Mum reading. She catches my look and I see the sadness in her. I sleep to the rocking of the train as we speed under the inky black western sky.

Duke gets a lesson

'Git here, ya bastard! Block up! Git behind!'

I'm in the cow paddock with Dukey and I'm trying to teach him to work cattle.

'Git here, you black bastard!'

All the shearers call their dogs 'black bastards' regardless of the colour.

He looks at me like I'm a stranger.

He is part labrador and part dalmation, which means he is fat with spots. He isn't black, though, which may be the cause of his confusion.

'Come here to me!'

Dukey looks dreamily at a cow.

'Skitch 'em!' I yell.

He moves sideways on his broad bum and snaps at a fly.

'Git behind!'

His tongue falls from the side of his mouth.

The cows eat themselves forward.

'Skitch 'em up!' I yell again.

He farts, and his tongue retreats and falls from the other side of his mouth.

I sit down heavily in the soft clover.

He comes to me, everything behind his head wagging, like he's suddenly recognised me in a crowd. I hold his head softly in my hands; he's no kelpie, that's for sure, and for now the cattle are safe. He rests his head on my shoulder and snuffles into my ear. He's glad I'm home and so am I.

We all have our places, the ones that speak to us when we're alone.

Big school

I started at Wyong High with a reputation as a killer, a knuckle man, someone not to be taken lightly; a man to be feared. It couldn't have been further from the truth. The reputation belonged to my brother who had finished high school the year before I arrived.

In Richard it was all true and deserved. He was undefeated. He didn't ever go looking for a fight – he was by nature gentle – but they came to him. Box-headed, big-boned kids from vacant farms. All the would-bes used to test their skills against him. One by bloodied one they were dispatched, done and dusted.

So here I am, on my first day of high school, with a new Globite case full of sharpened pencils, a wooden ruler, neat exercise books, a protractor, a peanut-butter sandwich and a bad reputation. I am wearing grey shorts, with sharp creases. I have a short-sleeved sky-blue shirt, and a burgundy-coloured school blazer with a crest on the pocket. The crest has a shield on it with a ladder that runs on the diagonal with the Latin *Tentando Superabis* across the top.

I am standing in the boys' toilet block.

I take a sip of water from the tap over the stainless-steel basin.

I pretend it's lemonade.

My stomach somersaults.

I look at myself in the mirrors above the basin and, even if I squint, there is nothing about me that says 'killer' – nothing.

I clench my buttocks tightly and make my way to the exit with my too-big case bumping against my knees.

I bump down a crowded corridor. Everything smells like chalk. I reach into my pocket and feel the knot in my hanky that has my bus money in the corner of it. Mum put it there early this morning. I think of Mum and the awkward warmth of her, of Dukey the dog and the cows eating themselves forward at home.

In the glare of the quadrangle, I haul the Globite into a space in the line among the jostling group of 1Bs. The crowd quiets as Mr Egger, the headmaster, coughs into a black microphone. I feel a little sweaty. He welcomes everyone back to the start of what he thinks will be another great year for Wyong High. I hear nothing of what he says. I finger the bus money again and think of Mum. Maybe I'm coming down with scarlet fever and I'll have to have six months off school, and I'll come back a hero having survived it.

I cough into my hanky to see if it sounds real, which causes the bus money to fall out and bounce in several directions at once. I bend over and lurch forward in an attempt to catch the coins. The sudden exertion caused by a rapid sequence of cough, bend and lurch causes my bowels to loosen and something warm squirts into my undies. Meanwhile the coins have disappeared under a sudden heap of excited kids.

I'm about to cry when somebody shouts, 'What's that smell? Poo!' and 'It's him, he's shat himself!' Suddenly the neat lines have dissolved into a frenzy as kids retreat from the source of the stench – me. The stress of it all has now caused the small stain in the rear of my shorts to widen, as several more squirts have now formed a stream. The commotion has caused the prefects and teachers to descend. I am now standing alone with a widening moat of emptiness around me. Kids are pointing at me with outstretched arms like spears, chanting 'Pooey! Pooey!'

I am bundled away at arm's length to the sick bay. I am cleaned up, my new shorts are washed and I am given a replacement pair from the lost-property bin. I lie on the bed while the school nurse is summoned.

There is a figure of Jesus on the wall opposite; he doesn't look well either. His thorny head is turned to one side and something is leaking out of the side of him. I know how he feels.

My stomach clenches and I dive for the bucket that has been placed beside the bed. There is sudden confusion in the hall outside the sick bay and now the room is filling with other kids in various states of distress. The nurse arrives with a local doctor in tow. I am joined at the bucket by another kid, whose spasms seem to be equal to if not worse than mine. Now there are kids hurling all over the place as every container halfway suitable is being used to contain the spill. I shoot a glance towards Jesus, who seems to be looking at something in the sky or at least on the ceiling. The nurse now looks like she's been hit and the doctor is doing his best to restore some order.

One hundred and twelve kids went down that day when an epidemic of gastroenteritis hit Wyong High School. It may not have been scarlet fever, but after a week off to recover I did come back a hero – because of the twenty-eight kids who'd shat themselves, I was the first, and I wore it like a prefect's badge, a badge of honour.

Back to school

I *really* don't know if I returned to school a hero but it felt like I had survived something. No one ever mentioned the poo episode, no one. I think it was one of those things that was too in your face, too big. If I had been the only one involved, the bullies would have had a field day. But as it stood, they were quietened by the sheer size of it and the weight of numbers of the victims. Occasionally I'd bump into someone in the playground who had been affected on that day and there would be something that passed between us, a silent recognition of something that we shared, another secret.

So here I was, turning another page in my book.

Despite my inauspicious start, after a week at high school I loved it.

I loved being in 1B. 1A was full of eggheads and geeks. Too much intelligence can make a person dull and unattractive. Geeky boys with big heads and glasses and pale skin from too much time spent indoors reading. The girls in 1A were the same: big brains, straight hair and a bit gawky. They seemed so concerned with the pursuit of knowledge that it drained them of spontaneity and life.

1B was different. We may have sat a few rungs lower on the IQ scale, but we excelled at the unbridled pursuit of fun.

I don't know how it happened, but over time I became part of a gang. By gang, I don't mean tough guys; we just sort of gravitated together. What a bunch! There was Gary Attenborough, with the biggest smile in the world, a fierce fighter who would never back down, a major defender of the gang. Robert Ehlein, a smooth operator, a leader with the gift of the gab, a lady-killer. Dicky Dunn was like a gunslinger without the guns: a cool guy, funny, and the first to try everything. I don't know what I was doing there – just telling stories as usual, I suppose.

We hung out at recess and lunchtime, played handball, mucked around down the oval, combed our hair a lot. There were lots of fights, country boys blowing off steam. You could feel it in the playground: a push, a shove back, the wrong word and – bang! And the chant would go up: Fight! Fight! No one ever got really hurt. At worst someone might end up with a bloody nose or a black eye, but it was mostly over quickly. I wasn't a good fighter. I was scared of the blood and I didn't want to hurt anybody.

Subject matter

As far as the laws of mathematics refer to reality,
they are not certain; and as far as they are certain,
they do not refer to reality.

Albert Einstein

I hated maths.

To make twelve-year-olds sit in a classroom for six hours a day is criminal enough, without subjecting them to the sheer lunacy of logarithms, algebra and the square root of anything.

In my adult life I have never had cause to put x over anything or y over anything else, nor do I have the slightest interest in finding out what would happen if I did. What a waste of precious time! Why not teach us something we could actually use, like foreplay? I could add and subtract, multiply and divide, but the moment the word *pi* was written on the blackboard a switch in my head would click into the off position and the one beside it that said 'daydream' would flick on and I was off somewhere, far away from the classroom, only to return when the large bell in the hall outside rang and put an end to the lunacy. I had better things to do with my time!

Science was more of a laugh. We thought quarks were the noises ducks made when you shot them.

Dark matter lived in your sister's armpit.

Genes were what you wore to the disco.

And a fossil was someone over forty.

Don't get me wrong – I really enjoyed science. Making rotten-egg gas in the lab, Bunsen burners and beakers with strange vapours leaking from them. Dissected frogs with electrodes clipped to their tiny bodies, which twitched when we hit the switch. You didn't need a book to tell you that man had descended from the apes. You could see that down the oval when the A-grade rugby team practised.

Atoms splitting, amoebas, the distance of planets from the sun, from us, from each other, lunar phases, Homo sapiens, Homo erectus, origin of the species, biodiversity, biosphere and on and on.

The biggest challenge I found in science was lugging the two huge blue textbooks around. They weighed a ton and just getting them to and from school was a major achievement, one guaranteed to turn you from Homo erectus to Homo bentoverus before you could say, 'Quark! There goes another duck!'

But if I was to get anything worthwhile out of my education, I needed to find something I was good at, something that would sustain me in the school years ahead. English saved me. My first poem was printed in the school magazine of 1963, my first year at high school.

TWENTIETH-CENTURY WAR

The sickle lies idle.
No laughter rings pure.
The dead all lie lonely,

Mind bent.

The clash of cold steel rings loud in the soul,

The fury of battle echoes the fear.

It was my reaction to the war in Vietnam. I think the best thing about it is the title.

Love on the silver screen

From the age of ten, I was allowed to catch the bus to Wyong to go to the Saturday matinee at the pictures. My parents would give me ten bob, which covered the return ticket on the bus, the admission to the theatre and a drink. It always felt special, going to the movies in the middle of the day. It felt like a guilty pleasure. I'd meet up with some mates and we'd all sit together, close. It was one of the first experiences I had when I really thought my parents were allowing me some independence. That they trusted me.

There would always be a newsreel to start with, covering some major events from home and abroad. The voice of the narrator was British and proper and made everything sound really important. Then there would be the cartoons, *Tom and Jerry* or *Bugs Bunny*. The serial came next. My favourite was

Flash Gordon. Ol' Flash would get into all sorts of trouble, usually trying to help a girl. Some villain would have tied her to the train tracks, the train would be coming fast, or she'd be tied to a bench in a sawmill with the giant blade inching closer and closer, then Ol' Flash would arrive, his dark eyes smouldering. At the very last moment, as the train was bearing down or the blade was about to tear into her milky white flesh, the words we knew were coming would flash across the screen: TO BE CONTINUED! And we'd be back again next week to see how Ol' Flash was going to get out of this one. After the serial had finished there would be an intermission and then the feature would start.

I loved the westerns. John Wayne as Davy Crockett in *The Alamo*, with Richard Widmark as the legendary Jim Bowie, who had a hunting knife named after him. Leading a bunch of Texan volunteers, they defended a mission just outside San Antonio against the Mexicans. I don't know how many westerns I saw, but not one featured a nice Mexican. They were all bastards! They had huge moustaches with bits of their last two meals sucked through them. They grinned like fools and they were all a bit on the tubby side (it was probably the beans). All they ever did was rape and pillage. John Wayne and the other Texans shot about a million of them, but they just kept coming, grinning like fat fools.

Westerns generally ran along the same lines. Most times it was the Indians who took a beating. They'd be whooping it up at night, dancing and drinking fire water and painting their bodies, preparing for the next day's battle against some cavalry outfit. They'd have a white woman tied to a pole in some chief's sweat lodge, the rawhide biting deep into her porcelain skin. A really ugly Indian brave with blue-black hair and a tomahawk would lurch into her teepee, eyes blazing and crazy drunk, and just as he was about to have him some of that white 'poontang', there would be the unmistakable sound of a Winchester rifle being cocked as Big John Wayne stepped out of the shadows. Later that night, as they made their getaway on stolen Navajo ponies and as the big ol' Texan moon shone down over the panhandle, she took him between her sweet thighs. It was her way of saying thank you. She thanked him a lot over the coming days.

*

I had my first real date at the Wyong pictures. It was a Saturday night. I had asked Barbara Dunstan, a girl from my class, if she would like to come with me. Well, I didn't actually ask her – I asked a friend of hers if she thought Barbara liked me. The friend thought she did but wasn't sure how much. A couple of days later, I heard that she'd said to someone that she did like me, but wasn't sure if she'd be allowed to come to the flicks. Messages were sent through trusted intermediaries and on the Friday morning at recess I was handed a crumpled note. It read:

Roses are red,
Violets are blue,
If you're going to the flicks,
I'll come with you.

Bingo!

I started to get ready on Saturday afternoon. I borrowed some of my brother's aftershave (nicked it, actually). I washed my ears out with a flannel from the bathroom. I cut my toenails and tipped baby powder down my undies. I made sure I had matching socks on. I polished my shoes till my arms ached. I covered my acne with Clearasil. Mum had made me a new red jerkin; it was like a vest but groovier. I put on my best white shirt, black pants, a thin black tie and the red jerkin, and slipped a freshly ironed hanky (with 'S' embroidered in one corner) in my pocket. I was set to go.

I caught the bus that got me to Wyong on the dot of seven. The bus stop was right out the front. I took a deep breath and got off. There she is, exactly where she said she would be, and even at a distance I can tell she is blushing. I am too, my face hot and prickly. There are lots of kids from school mingling and adults buying tickets. I make my way over to Barbara. We stand together, sort of. Neither of us speaks.

I finally ask her if she likes maths; she says no. I ask her if she has a ticket; she says no. I buy two from the ticket window and a small bucket of popcorn, and we go in.

'Hey, Bizo!' yells a mate from school. 'You and Barbara, eh? Woohoo!'

There are lots of couples. Some are pashing openly, some just lounging; they all look comfortable and relaxed. Barbara and I sit stiffly in our seats. Finally the theatre darkens and the newsreel begins. I know I have to do something, but I don't know what. I rack my brains. I've got it! I'll put my arm around her! I'll do it when I see a red car on the screen. The next time I see a red car I'll put my arm around Barbara Dunstan.

There's a problem. The newsreel's in black and white. I think some more. Okay, the next time I hear the word 'yesterday' I'll do it. The newsreel comes to an end, two tomorrows but no yesterdays. I remember I have the popcorn. I reach for it on the floor, and knock the box over in my scramble to pick it up because my hands are trembling so much. By the time I come up empty the cartoons have started. It's *Goofy* – not the one in the seat beside Barbara; the Walt Disney one, on the screen. The longer my indecision goes on, the harder it is to commit to anything. I know Barbara Dunstan wants me to put my arm around her, I can feel her whole mind, body and soul willing me in the dark of the theatre. 'Do it, do it,' chants the inside of me. 'Do it, do it,' answers the inside of Barbara Dunstan.

Suddenly I hear the word, as clear as a bell on a cow at dusk: 'yesterday'. A call to arms! My brain has taken control, a miniature electrical spark lights up a corner of the hippocampus, the current courses through myriad spidery networks, things go crack and pop and the signal surges to the muscles in my right arm.

It may have been that the strength of the signal from the brain was too much, as rather than encircling her in a soothing embrace, my arm flung sideways and caught her on the soft curve of her jawline, travelled on unimpeded to hit the flesh of her ear, before my flailing hand shot straight past the back of her head to strike an elderly woman in the row behind us on the knee. My head snapped to the right and even in the dark, Barbara's startled face shone like a beacon on a distant shore, and behind her and a little to her right another beacon, this one older, but no less startled.

My mouth had shaped to say something, but my brain was still struggling with the last bit and hadn't caught up. I made a noise like *harrumph*, which meant nothing to any of us, and bolted to the exit. I didn't stop running till I got to the milk co-op.

There were no buses to Lake Munmorah for another two hours, so I walked the fifteen miles home.

Cracker night

At the start of November each year, when summer had settled on the district, we had Cracker Night at our farm. We invited all the locals. For months before, we worked on building a huge bonfire in the middle of one of the paddocks. We dragged dead and dying branches from the surrounding bush. Fallen trees were stacked onto the ever growing heap. Worn tyres were flung and drums of diesel were poured over the lot. Finally we made a Guy Fawkes figure out of rags and hessian and sat him on top.

We spent every spare penny on crackers. Every newsagent in the big towns had fireworks for sale. They all looked so beautiful in their brightly covered wrappers. There were skyrockets with long sticks, Catherine wheels that spun and sputtered with bright sparks flying as they whirled. Cone-shaped crackers that blew coloured balls high into the air. But best of all were the bungers! There were the bright red penny bungers and fat tuppenny ones, each with a drooping wick that hung from the top, just waiting for the match. We'd take them to the creek, light the wick then throw them deep into the water and wait for the *wump* to come. If you threw too soon, the water extinguished the wick and ruined the bunger; too late and you risked it going off in your hand or, worse still, beside your ear as you lifted your arm to throw – *boom!* – and your ears would be ringing for a week.

We put them under metal garbage bin lids and blew them high into the sky. We made cracker guns: a length of water pipe with one end sealed and a hole for the wick to come through. You slid the cracker into the pipe, fed the wick through the hole and dropped a marble into the pipe, lit the wick and aimed it. Deadly.

My Uncle George from across the creek started the bonfire. He first drenched the heap with a mixture of petrol and gunpowder then poured a trail from the heap to the beer tent. He struck a match and lit the end of the trail. A great arrow of fire shot through the paddock and the heap virtually exploded. The Guy Fawkes figure on top shot a hundred feet into the air then fell to earth in a shower of sparks. Luckily, it didn't hit anyone. People did go a bit nuts on Cracker Night. Maybe it was the danger. There was the reek of gunpowder, the rockets screeching through the sky and exploding overhead, the showers of gold raining down, the bungers exploding ...

Even Dad went a bit crazy. One Cracker Night I saw him standing on the toilet roof, he had one of my mother's dresses on and he was fully made up and, when any of the women went in, he'd throw bungers in through the windows – only small ones, but enough to frighten the hell out of them.

He didn't really need to throw the bungers, just the look of him in the dress was frightening enough. The weird thing was, he was the only one in fancy dress.

We'd get up early the next morning and scour the paddocks for the unexploded crackers and for weeks after Cracker Night the valley resounded to the sounds of small explosions.

The Wyong Show

There's a bull with a brass ring in its nose.

There are blokes selling shiny tractors to other blokes who can't afford 'em.

In the produce pavilion there's a perfect pear in a glass jar and a giant pumpkin.

There's a bloke selling car-seat covers and a knife that will cut through a brick and then slice a tomato into perfect quarters.

There are bright-eyed kelpies driving three tired sheep up a race.

There are blokes getting thrown off bulls that weigh a ton at the rodeo in the main arena.

Kids with painted faces suck the life from watery snow cones.

There's fairy floss.

There are scones with clotted cream and jam on top.

Pluto pups with greasy batter and sauce.

Blokes in sandshoes cut their weight in wood.

There's a bloke in a kilt trying to find a band, and a copper with a lost kid.

There are clowns down in sideshow alley. Their gaping mouths swing from side to side waiting for the next kid with the grimy ping-pong balls to have a go. 'Every kid wins a prize!'

There are bullet-ridden tin ducks next door at the shooting gallery, with slug guns all in a row at the front. There's a wall of furry animals at the back, dusty from too many shows.

At the knock-'em-downs I got a tin clicker with a grasshopper painted on the back for knocking over three cans with two balls, when what I really wanted was the spud gun on the second row.

I click my way deeper into the alley. There are blokes with ruddy faces yelling "Ave a go'; women with weathered bodies take the cash for keeps.

I meet some mates and we slink off to the place we really want to be: THE STRIP SHOW. There are girls on a platform out the front with sequined bras and long legs in high-heeled shoes and veils, lots of veils. You hardly ever see anyone wearing a veil, only at weddings and strip shows, really. The spruiker says, 'You'll see it all inside.' We edge to the ticket window. The woman behind the glass says, 'I hope you're old enough?' and slides the tickets to us, knowing we're not. We're not, not by a long shot. We bolt for the tent. Inside it's jammed full of blokes, sweating and jostling for a better view, the air thick with the smell of stale beer, BO and fags.

There is a small stage at the front with a sparkly curtain. Music leaks from a battered speaker. It feels naughty in here and hot and sweaty. My breath is suddenly ragged. The speaker crackles and a raspy male voice says, 'Put your hands together for the lovely, the sexy, the beautiful Lolita! And remember, youse blokes – no touching!'

Raunchy music blares from the speaker as the curtains open. Lolita stands in the middle of the stage. I try to think of ice and polar bears to settle myself as I stare at her. I just stare. She begins to dance, her long white legs set wide as she gyrates on the small stage. I try to think of water and calm and goodness, but all I get is the smell of musk sticks and juice.

She runs her long fingers along the length of each leg, over her flat stomach to linger on the curve of her full breasts. I can't think … of anything. She slides one long finger between the red slash of her full lips and sucks on it, sucks it deep inside her, and grins. I can smell the scent of her body from where I stand. It's rich and dark and musky and sticky and hot. It is all over me and through me. I look around to see if others have noticed, but they're all transfixed like me and flustered to a man, cherubic faces upturned, all flushed cheeks and sweat and something like innocence.

She shimmies, she struts. A brassy saxophone growls from the guts of the speaker and the tent trembles in the heat. She is magnificent! She reaches behind her slender back and unclips her bra. Our Father, who art in Heaven … The sparkly top falls to the floor and she is naked from the waist up. Naked. She stands in front of us and silently dares us to look away, and nobody does. Nobody in that musky tent in the middle of the Wyong showground on a hot February afternoon does anything but stare. One half-nude woman holds fifty men and three boys spellbound and dares them to move, and nobody does until the saxophone dies and the sparkly curtain closes.

We head from the tent into the bright glare. We stand in a loose group too shaken to speak till Brooksey croaks, 'Let's get a Coke,' and we're off, released and fired up. We bump into my brother. He's with his friends, big guys. They've been in the beer tent 'cause they're old enough. Some have girls with them. Babes, all net dresses and beehive hairdos. Richard's with his new girlfriend, Lisabeth; she's from Swansea and works in the cake shop.

'Been to the strip show yet?' says Rich.

'No way, not old enough,' I say, but my mate Wayney bursts out laughing and I know we've been sprung.

'Did ya get a stiffy?' says Clarky, one of my brother's mates.

I did, but then I'd had one for the last two years, more or less. Mostly more. Someone tells Clarky to get fucked and we're gone. We pick up the Cokes and head to the arena. I've still got the stiffy, but I'm used to it.

There are blokes in hats leading squat cows around.

There are blokes following the cows around with shovels, scooping up the shit.

I wonder how many years the bloke on the shovel's got to do before he gets a go at leading the cow.

We find a spot and settle in. We talk about what we could have done to Lolita and what she could have done to us. That takes about an hour and I've got another stiffy or maybe it's the same one, it's hard to tell. We head off to the dodgems and crash and bump for a while. I lose the stiffy on the next ride, the Go-Go, from being whirled around so fast – or maybe it was the spewing that did it. Either way, it's gone and that's a relief. Sort of.

We head up sideshow alley and bump into three girls from our school: Judy Long, who sounds like a Pom and everyone reckons is a goer; Michelle Gribble; and Cathy Forrest, a blonde. I love blondes. Cathy is all body; there's so much of it that it's hard to take it all in. She's like a junior Lolita, but local. We circle them in some vague pincer movement. It's a stand-off. They all look so wrong out of uniform, all hairspray and bows. The smell of their perfume arrives about a minute later and falls on us like bricks. The lipstick needs work as well.

'Where youse goin'?' asks Judy.

'Anywhere you are,' says Dave.

'Yeah! Let's go on the Rotor so we can see your panties,' says Brooksey.

I agree with everyone.

'*Then* what are you gunna do?' Cathy wants to know.

Brooksey holds his ground. 'You'll see!'

We head up the alley. It's on. We wait in line. It takes three more sessions to finally empty the queue and suddenly we're in. It's like being in a barrel that's standing on one end with its lid cut off. We line the curved walls, facing inwards, our arms outstretched as the barrel begins to spin. Now the speed comes on fast and things begin to blur and bleed. The girls are opposite, hair like sea grass, moving, clothes sucked to their bodies. The floor jolts beneath our feet as they start to lower it. It starts to go; the girls scream. 'Shit!' yells Brooksey. The floor is now six feet below and dropping fast as we whirl.

I look to my left at Dave, who's turned himself upside down, his face contorting from the force. Brooksey's gone as white as a sheet and the girls are all screaming for real. Cathy's top has crept up. She catches me looking and doesn't try to pull it back down. Jesus, she's beautiful. I decide I'm going to ask her to come on the ghost train with me. There are people watching from above. Someone wolf-whistles and I bet it's for Cathy. Who else? There's just too much of her. The ride starts to slow and we all slip down the walls to the floor below. I help Cathy to her feet.

'Wanna go on the ghost train with me?' she asks, and takes my hand and leads me out into the sudden glory of sideshow alley.

Lord, if you let me live for the next ten minutes, I will serve you till Eternity, I think.

We ride the ghost train six times. It is the day I learn to kiss better. The day the earth moves, sideways.

We leave the ride in a daze and just cruise through the show. I don't know what I feel, and I don't care. I kiss her about another thousand times. She says she has to go find her friends 'cause we'd given them the slip. Can we meet up for the fireworks at eight? She goes. My lips feel like they've been through a cheese grater. They've never felt better.

I decide to go for a wander. I hope I don't bump into anyone I know for a while, 'cause I'm still in the glow. That's the only way I can describe it: a soft warm glow. I head back up the alley past the stupid clowns. The spud gun is still on the second shelf at the shooting gallery; I'll come back later for another crack at it. I pass a show for littlies called *Snow White*. There's a group of women out the front with prams and snotty-nosed kids. Up on the raised platform is a girl in a long red dress and a bad wig with a bunch of dwarves around her. Dopey's picking his nose, Sleepy's having a fag and Grumpy looks a bit pissed. I drift along. Past the half-man, half-woman show, which I'd been to last year. It was crap – just some poof in half a frock and half a dinner suit sewn together, with short hair on one side of his head and half a wig on the other. There's a two-headed calf, a dog that can sing and a bloke that can swallow glass.

It's just weird shit down here.

'Hey, Bizo!' It's Dicky Dunn, the gunslinger. He's got so many loves bites on his neck that his head could fall off any minute. 'Saw you on the ghost train, mate, with Cathy!'

'So?'

'Did ya get a look at her tits?'

Word travels fast around here. It turns out he's been working on the ghost train, poking people with a plastic skeleton hand for five bob an hour. He says that if he has to clean up any spew he gets an extra bob. 'Sounds great!' I say. He says he'll see if he can get me some work as well. I tell him I have to meet Cathy later, so I'll have to pass. He heads back to work and I drift.

I'm just tossing up whether I'll go and catch Col Joye and the Joy Boys at the music tent when I see Dave heading towards me in a rush.

'Bizo!' he yells. 'Where ya been? Been looking for you everywhere! Your brother's gunna have a go at the boxing tent!'

By the time we arrive there's a massive crowd out the front. Jimmy Sharman, the owner and showman, is up on the platform revving up the crowd.

'Come up here, local fella, come up here and have a go! Come up here if ya think yer good enough!'

There must be a dozen of Jimmy's fighters on the stand. Their shiny robes flutter and twirl around them as they shadow-box, left, right, the short jab and the lethal uppercut, slicing the air as they dance. They move like fluid shadows, these black boys. They've fought in every backwater in the country against all comers. There's jet-black fellas from the Territory and square-jawed whitefellas from towns and broken farms, the dirt still in them.

'I heard you Wyong boys are as weak as piss!' growls Jimmy.

A roar goes up from the crowd.

Jimmy stokes the fire. 'Well, if you local blokes aren't as weak as piss, then come up here and have a go!'

There's a black fighter on the end with a bass drum. He starts the *boompah, boompah* beat while another rings a clanging bell. Now the fighters from the troupe start to challenge blokes in the crowd.

'Hey you, baldy, come up here – I'll 'ave ya!'

More taunts follow and the crowd roars the insults back. Jimmy's got them right where he wants them and finally up they come, the local boys, led by my brother. Richard, with the gentle heart and the soft brown eyes. He's obviously been at the beer tent since I bumped into him earlier in the day. I don't think he'd have been a starter without the fortification. Not that he's scared; he's a renowned fighter. I've seen him go, and he's good, very good.

Jimmy Sharman sorts who's going to fight who. Richard is paired with a black fighter and once all the other matches are set the crowd surges into the tent. They want blood, and they don't really care who it comes from. Inside is the vacant ring, fresh bloodstains on the canvas and the grimy ropes slack and drooping.

There's a bloke waiting in one of the corners for the fighters to glove up. His face is a mess. What's left of his nose is spread and flattened across a pockmarked face. His ears are gristly and his teeth are mostly missing, and he's just the referee.

The fighters enter the ring. There will be three three-minute rounds, and if the local bloke wins he gets ten quid. The crowd sizes up the fighters and the side bets go on. There are blokes with fistfuls of money trying to get others to take the bet. 'Ten quid on the boong !' and 'I'll take it, over here!' and 'I got twenty says the whitey won't make it past the second!' 'Bullshit – you're on!'

The bell rings and the fighters join the ref in the middle.

'Keep it clean, no biting, no low punches and break when I tell ya!'

They retreat to the neutral corners.

Ding-ding goes the bell and it's on. The local bloke is first out to the middle and he looks impressive, fast hands, good balance. They circle each other, the punches probing, searching, measuring the distance to the strike zone. The black fighter is coiled like a spring, his hands low, his chin jutted like an invite. The local bloke takes the bait and throws a looping left at the target. The black spring uncoils, the head ducks as he steps inside and unleashes the deadly right in a blur of speed and power. The white guy's brain turns into an instant kaleidoscope of colour and bright light. He remembers a picnic with a girl on a beach … somewhere, and the sound of soft rain, falling, falling. His legs are working on a vague memory of balance which can't last, and doesn't. The black fighter gets to him fast, claims him in a safe embrace and lowers him gently to the canvas. 'Piss weak!' yells some fool.

Money changes hands in the crowd. They wake the local bloke with smelling salts and care. He used to think he was a fighter and for twenty-three seconds he was.

My brother steps into the ring. His bare torso, white under the light, is thickset and muscled, his dark eyes fixed and determined. I've seen this purpose in him before. There's no bluster about him, nothing showy, just the need to finish what's been started. His opponent steps through the ropes. He's blacker than the first fighter, leaner and taller than my brother by a foot.

They join the ref in the middle for the muttered instructions.

'Come on, Dick, get into him!' yells a mate, thinking it might help.

The fighters retreat.

The bell clangs.

The black bloke's done this a hundred times before, faced off against whoever, wherever. He's saving up to go back to Broome, maybe go pearl diving, or buy a tinnie and go fishing with his cousin Arnold for a living. He thinks of the breeze across Roebuck Bay. The kapok trees flowering now, big mob of crocodile eggs. A girl, tall one, waiting there now.

The punches fizz around his head.

Bang! One gets through.

He's back now, in a tent, in a fight, somewhere in New South Wales.

He'd kill for a barra.

I can't remember every punch, but I know I prayed for the third time that day. I can't even remember what I said in the prayer, though I'm pretty sure it sounded as lame as the other two, unconvincing. I don't know much about religion but I know you've really got to sell a prayer. You've got to at least pretend you believe, otherwise you won't stand a chance of it getting through to the guy with the red face.

They punch on for three rounds, and in the end it's a draw. Richard gets five quid and the black bloke gets a feed.

I come out of the tent into the twilight. I see my brother surrounded, heading back to the beer tent. What a day! What an absolute corker of a day. Lust and blood and fairy floss!

I meet up with Cathy later, and we find a quiet spot on a broken hay bale behind the chook pavilion. She smells like boiled lollies. The fireworks go off. You see, it's true – at the show, everyone's a winner!

Gypsies and other strangers

There are Cadillacs on the highway coming south! Sleek low riders with pedestrian-killer fins, Chevys with thumping V8s towing sleek silver vans. Chopped-top Customlines, DeSotos and Pontiacs.

The gypsies are coming!

We didn't like foreigners.

People locked their doors and kept their children close. They were coming all right! Someone had seen them in Swansea that morning, fuelling the big American cars. They swore there were twenty in the convoy at least.

Blokes on farms locked the shed.

Their wives hid their jewellery.

Better safe than sorry was the word.

The gypsies were here!

They were true nomads. They had to be. They'd been running for a thousand years. Word had it that they had originated in India when the Islamic invaders had expelled them. They had been persecuted throughout Europe for hundreds of years as they searched for a place to settle and to rest.

In Australia they followed the harvest season down the east coast, fruit picking and doing general farm work. They worked the show and carnival circuits. They were skilled horse-breakers and metal workers. But whatever their skills, they weren't welcome here.

There was a large tract of open land just off the highway only a mile from our place. They circled the flashy American cars like they had their wagons in olden times. At night the cooking fires blazed as they sang the songs of old to the strains of the accordion, fiddle and drum. They danced and sang under the stars, barefoot and free. They always stayed a week. They would visit the local farms in search of work. They would offer to bless money or cast spells to ward off sickness or poverty. They were physically striking: dark-skinned with hooded blue eyes. The women had an exotic beauty about them, slim and lithe. The men were muscular and quick and the kids were like dark cherubs, beautiful but different, strange.

We feared them.

We locked our doors against them and lay in our safe beds at night, in our safe houses, and told ourselves that they were thieves and tricksters. In truth, what we feared was our own small lives and the freedom we knew they had. When they had gone we would tell ourselves that we were safe now, safe like before.

We were white and we were Australians.

We didn't even like Poms, and we were descended from them.

We didn't really like anybody.

There was a local Aboriginal man who lived in a humpy on a small plot of land. He did odd jobs around the place; there wasn't much he couldn't do. He was a skilled horse-breaker. He had a way with horses that was amazing to watch. He would walk into a paddock full of horses and just stand there unmoving. One by one they would come to him, and when they did he would move away. Again and again they would follow. He would run from them and they would chase him, just to be near him. He would whisper secret things in their ears and blow his calming breath into their wide nostrils.

He would work all day for you, he never made demands, he broke all our horses in – but you never took him to the pub or had him in your house, because at the end of the day he was just a blackfella, a boong, a coon.

Italians were wogs or dagos. Sometimes we called them Eye-ties. They were mad for a tomato. I've never known another race of people that were so crazy for a vegetable like Eye-ties were for a tomato, never. They worshipped tomatoes. They made sauce out of them. They put them on the base of their pizzas, cut them up and put them on bread, boiled them, dried them, puréed and mashed them.

I had a mate at school who was a dago. I was round at his place one Saturday morning when all his rellos arrived. Everyone had brought tomatoes with them. Paolo's parents grew more stuff in their small backyard than we grew on our entire farm. There were grapes growing across the patio out the back, rows of climbing peas and beans along the fence. Pumpkins and melons fought each other like gangs, their twisted tendrils interwoven. There were rows of corn and carrots, great clumps of beetroot, garlic and onions and potatoes in the dark earth. There were pots of chilli like firecrackers and pendulous sweet peppers, languid in the heat. Cucumber and zucchini, lettuce and leeks, ran riot, and everywhere *pomodoro*, the love apple.

There must have been a dozen kinds. Some squat and pillar-box red, others the colour of port wine, elegant romas hanging, the trestles bending with the weight of them, and potted types, small and zesty – and everywhere the sweet, acrid smell of them.

More dagos arrive, and suddenly there's food everywhere. Great doughy loaves of crusty bread, oily olives in olive oil, homemade salami and prosciutto, great wedges of cheese, wine from cousin Fredo in last year's bottles, *ragù* Bolognese and everything laid out on scrubbed tables under the vines. We ate for hours. This wasn't a party; this was a family having lunch together on a Saturday.

After lunch, with the tables cleared, the work began.

The tomatoes were all put into wooden fruit boxes for ease of handling and stacked at the end of one of the tables. I sat with Paolo and some of the bigger kids. We were each given a knife and a cutting board. Our job was to cut the tomatoes into rough quarters. Fires were lit and huge pots set over the flames till the water frothed and boiled. Fresh herbs were cut from the garden and cast into the pots with handfuls of coarse salt. Some of the fruit was left whole and put into a separate pot, to later have their loosened skins removed and finally made into a paste-like concentrate, preserved in oil to be used in the months ahead. Nothing wasted, everything precious, everything shared.

Our quartered fruit was tipped into the waiting pots and boiled till they were reduced to a thick molten sauce, rich and blood red. When strained, preserved and bottled, the sauce would line the shelves in the kitchens of twenty families for the following year.

I rode my bike home in the late afternoon. I arrived home in time for dinner: curried mince on toast and a cuppa.

*

My sister had a Greek boyfriend for a while, Nick Something-opolous. All I knew about Greeks was they liked boats and fishing and they could dance, but only in a circle. This bloke's father owned Pete's Café in the main drag at Wyong. All the wogs in the district used to go there for the strange food. We used to go as well because they had a sign in the window that said AUSTRALIAN MEALS SERVED. They had the best mixed grill on the coast and the banana split was heaven in a bowl.

All the young Greek guys used to hang out there. They were known as rockers. The guys all wore black mesh T-shirts and black stovepipe jeans and ripple-soled shoes called 'brothel creepers'. Some wore shoes with points like knives. There were two long mirrors out the front. They'd be out there, legs spread wide, combing their hair into what was known as 'racks', the sides gleaming with Brylcreem and the middle section falling forward like two greasy waves to rest on their foreheads. They wore car badges for belt buckles. Their chicks wore tight dresses and black shit around their eyes and motorcycle jackets with their bras thrust out like cones. They drove American cars – Chevys, Ford Mustangs, Pontiacs and Oldsmobiles – or souped-up local jobs, Holdens,

Fords and Valiants. There would be fluffy dice hanging from the rear-view mirror and stickers on the back window saying *Moon equipped*. They rode motorbikes as well, Nortons, Ariels and BSAs.

The Chinese were called Chinks. The only Chinks I ever saw owned the Chinese restaurant in Wyong. We never went; we mistrusted the food. The only thing I knew about the Chinese was they invented fireworks and were good at ping-pong.

The local garage was owned by Dutch people. They had a sort of dum-de-dum way of speaking and wore weird shoes. Americans were only on TV and were the best at everything, ever. That was about it for foreigners – except for the Indians, who had wobbly heads, and the Japanese, who were still on detention because of the war.

Gangs

It's midnight, Saturday in Charmhaven.

A blot on a dot on a map of the coast. More fibro shacks, cacti, weeds and gravel, tinnies in the spare fridge and a boat rusting in the carport. On a clear day you can see the new power station across the lake. Problem is, the days are always clear. Seaweed flops on what used to be a beach. There was never weed here before they built the plant. Now there's more weed than water. The prawns have gone. Or gone somewhere.

The rockers are here. Greaseballs, some wogs, some whites, Elvis freaks and James Dean lookalikes. Fast cars parked under the only streetlight on the town side. Chicks with too much mascara sit close on the bench seats, short dresses, bad shoes, their panties on the floor by the stick shift. Bad girls with bad boys. Engines on nitro throb and suck the night air. Elvis on the eight track, daddy-o.

Five miles north and closing, the surfies are coming. Hair like tangled rope and the sea in their eyes. This meeting is no accident. It was settled a week ago. 'Midnight, Saturday, Charmhaven – be late, be dead.' Ten in the convoy and more if they're needed; we'll see when we get there. Someone heard a rumour about knives so tonight there are iron bars in the boot. It's all because of a girl, someone else's girl.

Mitch in the DeSoto three back from the lead. He's the one that did it. Pulled the rocker's girl in the pub a week ago, while her bloke was on shift down the mines. All's fair. And if tonight goes as planned he'll be doing it again, first chance he gets. If you'd seen her arse, you would too.

The convoy arrives and parks up. Motors growling, tyres spinning and smoking on the black stuff. Surfboards on racks on the roof. Dogs pissing on other dogs' scent and the bitches on heat in the dark cars. Then the quiet. Two gangs each side of the black road now, waiting for the next step, waiting for something to happen, for something to break.

Two interstates looming from the south. Air horns blaring from the lead rig cut the mood to the quick. Spotlights tear the night to ribbons and they're gone, barrelling to Brisbane on eighteen wheels and a pocketful of pills. His mate behind rants into the open channel of the CB about his cheating wife, too many mouths to feed, fucking hippies and the price of piss, pies and diesel. He's so wired, he followed an Alsatian from Yass to Goulburn earlier. He's looking for another one to get him to Kempsey. He's been amped for two days but needs this trip to make ends meet. His eyes are locked on the lead truck, his head full of demons and darkness.

Back at the Haven the wogs issue the challenge across the road.

'Youse rope-heads send your little mate over the road to apologise for what he done, otherwise …'

'Otherwise what?'

'Otherwise the bitch gets another hiding. I'll do it meself right here, right now!'

This is not about the girl.

It's just a way to get it started.

They think it's hate; it gives them a reason.

It's not that either.

It's not rockers against surfers, black against white, us against them or the wogs or the slopes, the chinks or the gooks.

It's as old as dirt itself.

It's about being recognised, for something, anything.

Making a mark.

It's about a release, the letting go of something deep. Something caught in the blood and feeling it loosen and fighting and screaming with the rage of forcing it free.

Mitch undoes the buttons on his best shirt and strips to the waist. It was always going to come to this. He knows he won't be crossing the road alone; one in, all in, like always.

'Shhhh for a second!' someone says. 'Everyone just shut up for a minute.'

Now they all hear it, the sirens wailing in the night from the north, distant now but coming fast. 'It's Evans. Piss off or he'll lock you up.'

Someone's rung the cops in Swansea. Someone in a fibro house who pays their rates and puts up with this shit most Saturday nights. Someone who's had enough.

'You mullets, better be here next week or ...' The threat gets lost as the tyres squeal and smoke on the black stuff. Everyone's heading south, away from the threat. No one wants to be here when Evans turns up. No one's that stupid, they think. And anyway, there's always next week, and the one after that, and the one after that.

Two am in Charmhaven.

A blot on a dot on a map of the coast.

The lights on the power station wink across the weedy lake.

Big trouble

The headmaster's name is Mr Egger, so of course he's called 'the Goog'. The deputy headmaster is Mr Ferguson, known as 'Mousey' because he has the look of the rodent about him.

Gary Grant and me are standing outside the Goog's office, which can only mean one thing: trouble. I don't know why we're here and if Gary knows, he's not saying. I rack my brains to see if I can remember anything I might have done, but I come up empty. We've been summoned here from the first period after lunch. Earlier in the day we'd been given half a period off before the morning recess to prepare tea and biscuits in the teachers' staffroom. I'd done it several times before and it's a bludge.

I'd unpacked the biscuits and arranged them on a large white platter. There are twenty-five teachers and at two each, that's a lot of biscuits.

Gary was over by the sink filling the two large iron teapots from the silver urn and with twenty-five teachers, that's a lot of tea. The bell sounded to signal the start of recess. I quickly filled the two large glass jugs with milk from the fridge, placed them on the table and we were done and gone, easy.

We wait outside the office. Time saunters on. Maybe it's about the half-pack of Arrowroot biscuits we knocked off before we left the staffroom. No, couldn't be that. Who would have known? Who would have cared? I check my lips for crumbs.

'Bisley, Grant!' It's Mousey, the deputy, a small neat man. 'Inside!' Small and neat maybe, but vicious with the cane.

We go in. The Goog's at his desk, with a hand supporting his chin as he reads from a stack of papers. We stop in front of his large dark desk. Mousey stands beside Mr Egger. Bad cop, bad cop. The Goog reads on. More waiting, just like at home, in the shed.

School sounds leak into the office and swell and fade and swell again. The trill of a whistle from the oval, ten times tables droning in the distance, a door slamming somewhere and another somewhere else, magpies arguing in the trees outside the tuckshop and far off a clarinet played badly pipes and squawks to a thankful end.

The headmaster screws the lid on his delicate gold-tipped fountain pen and places it neatly beside the squat blue ink bottle, his fingers the colour of washed oysters, his nails trimmed to perfection. He slides the stacked papers sideways, leans back into the plush leather of the chair and stares at us.

Mousey cuts the silence like a rapier. 'You boys were assisting in the preparation of the teachers' morning tea today – is that correct, Bisley?'

'Yes, sir,' I reply, puzzled.

'You, Grant?'

'Sir?'

'You and Bisley were assisting in the preparation of the teachers' morning tea today, yes or no?'

I shoot a glance at Gary. His face is reddening and his gaze is fixed on a spot on the floor.

'Grant?'

Nothing.

I'm still looking at Gary and can't understand why he's not responding.

'Who made the tea?' asks the headmaster.

I wait.

Nothing from Gary!

'Bisley, who made the tea?'

'I did the biscuits,' I say.

Silence.

The bell sounds the end of the period, then the noise of the school moving from one classroom to another.

We wait. A small knock on the door. Mousey opens it. A muted conversation, the other voice a woman's, words short, sharp, to the point, the door closing with a sigh. Mousey turns from the door. He has one of the bright iron teapots in his hands, all wrong against his neat dark suit. He carries it like a trophy and places it squarely in the centre of the headmaster's desk then steps back.

'Lift the lid, Grant!'

Gary inches forward like something hobbled. His right hand hovers over the lid like a bird. Finally he lifts it clear and places it on the desk.

'What can you smell, Grant?' asks Mousey.

Nothing from Gary.

'I'll ask you again, Grant: what can you smell?'

Still nothing.

'Bisley, what can you smell?'

'Urine, sir!'

'Who pissed in the teapot?'

'I don't know, sir,' I say.

'You're excused, Bisley,' says Mr Egger.

I leave the office. It's like leaving a condemned man on death row. I can't even begin to understand why he did it. He must have known he'd be caught.

Maybe that was the point.

I'd been back in class for half an hour when Gary came back. He looked like he'd been crying and his hands were red from the cane. He didn't say anything; he just packed his bag and left without a look. I never saw him again.

Finding the light

It was the start of second term in first year when I was asked to join the organising committee, a group that was responsible for planning the social side of school life. The group was selected by the teaching staff and was made up of a student from each year from first year to fifth. We planned all the fetes, market days, dances and socials. We did everything from booking bands and decorating the school hall to arranging the catering and selling tickets. We were the major fundraising body of the school and the success or failure of each event rested on us. We were given some time off from class to handle our responsibilities – bliss. It was a gig everyone in the school wanted.

We had three market days a year. A market day was like a mini fete and was used to raise money for each of the school's four colour houses: Baker, McKimm, Allen and Rose. I was in Baker. Each house would have a number of stalls or events and the house that raised the most money was given a pennant and was applauded at the school assembly.

I created a sort of psychedelic club in one of the classrooms. We all sat around in what we thought were hippy-type clothes, with bare feet and flowers in our hair, and said, 'Peace, man,' a lot. We decorated the walls in wild fluoro colours from the art department. We charged two bob to come in. We played sitar music and sold watered-down cordial in cups. We were a huge hit and raised the most amount of money on the day. I had the best time!

I threw everything I had into the social side of school. At the committee meetings I was full of ideas of what bands we should have, how the hall should be decorated. I worked for months on plans for the end-of-year dance. In the final week it was a mad rush to decorate the hall and make sure we had done everything possible to make the night a success. On the night I was standing in the wings to one side of the stage as the band was playing, making sure that everything was all right backstage. I remember looking out at this sea of writhing teenagers and thinking to myself that this was something I would love to do with my life: to entertain, to move people somehow.

Chuck

I'll remember this day forever.

I've got a good memory. Sometimes it's a curse.

I remember what the light in the room was like the first time I heard Van Morrison's album *Moondance*.

I remember hearing the news of JFK's assassination on the school bus and how we were all completely numbed by it, even in Lake Munmorah.

I remember the taste of burnt cocoa on a camping trip.

Memories of kisses and love and rejection and loss and regret. Of bliss and hangovers and powder on old skin and my first car and the smell of it. Of fresh-mown grass and milk straight from the warm cow and a fart under a blanket leaking out. Chalky classrooms, wet dogs and the tingle of champagne on my tongue the first time. The smell of brass, sawn timber, burnt toast and the sweet smell of death and new shoes and shit and fear.

I'll remember this day forever.

It's late November 1963 and in less than a month I'll be a teenager.

The school bus stops at my road.

The smell of grease and diesel and dust.

It takes a thousand steps to get to the farm; I've counted every one of them. I start to the sound of bees in the new wattle and cicadas: black princes, green grocers, yellow Mondays and floury bakers droning in the bush. I walk on. There's been rain today and the clouds are in puddles in low spots on the road. I walk through two of them to feel the water flood my shoes and soak my feet. I smell the sweet sap from the gums in the steamy heat, halfway home now, five hundred steps to go. Sandy's house on the left, bare fibro walls and quiet, they're away doing God's work. Horse floats in the Nickelsons' yard and a black stallion cropping new shoots at the fence line pauses to watch me pass.

Uncle Roy, up a tall ladder spraying early peaches in the

Carters' neat orchard, waves with a free hand. Nectarines yellowing at the three hundred mark. Aunty Vi wrestling flapping sheets at the clothes line and it's all downhill from here. Through the gate into the yard and Dukey coming, wagging everything behind his head. Through the screen door into the cool of the kitchen for arvo tea.

'Mum?'

No answer. I know she's here; I can smell the chalk.

'Mum!'

Vegemite on a Sao.

'Mum!' Nothing.

Something has begun. Something dark.

I find her in her bedroom, perched on the end of the bed, a yellow manila envelope beside her. She looks straight ahead into the falling afternoon and the orchard. 'Your school report came home today … You'd better read it before your father comes home.' She leaves the room without a look.

I hear the pop from the sherry bottle opening and the liquor gurgling into a glass. She's already battening down the hatches. I pick up the envelope and carry it to my room. I take out the two white pages and read.

STEPHEN BISLEY 1B

English: Credit

Art: Pass

Geography: Fail

Maths: Fail

History: Fail

Science: Fail

COMMENTS

Stephen's results are disappointing. He has the ability to do much better, but needs to apply himself in all areas.

There's a man in a black Jaguar heading south on the Pacific Highway. He's been teaching others the things he can't teach us. He has a large silver handgun in the glove box of the car. He pulls over to the side of the road. The Jaguar idles in the falling light. He takes six brass-jacketed bullets from the pocket of his coat. Each bullet has my name etched deep into its bright casing. He feeds the bullets into the gaping chamber of the gun. He places the gun carefully back into the glove box and closes it. He hauls the sleek car back onto the road. He's coming.

*

I feed the death sentence back into the envelope.

Mum sits at the kitchen table.

I sit in my bedroom.

Mum sips the warm sherry.

I sit in my bedroom.

Chuck Yeager was an American pilot who tested the first jet-propelled aeroplane over the Mojave Desert in Southern California. They didn't quite know what was going to happen when they rolled it out of the hangar, pointed it down the runway and lit the wick. Sure, they had tested it on the ground and in wind tunnels and the like, but that's not the same.

Chuck's now at about fifty thousand feet above the ground, blistering the sky with the jet screaming, when the aerodynamics go all pear-shaped and the plane starts handling like a bunch of falling car keys and he runs out of options and finally has to eject. He wrenches open the canopy and hits the big red button on the dash. The canister under his seat explodes like it's meant to and blasts him clear of the plane.

To add to his problems, some of the burning propellant from the canister lodges inside his helmet and now he's falling to earth, struggling to get his chute to open with one side of his face on fire. Meanwhile the multi-million-dollar aircraft he has just abandoned crashes into the desert about a mile below him, making a hole about the size of the Superdome.

I sit on the bed with Chuck.

I've run out of options too.

Chuck leaves. I would too, but I've got nowhere to go.

It's too early but I change out of my school uniform into my pyjamas. They're blue and white and they make me look vulnerable and I think that might help. I hear the sound of the big black car on the downgrade into the yard, its tyres crunching on the gravel as it arcs into the carport.

I think of the revolver in the glove box, the bullets with my name engraved on them. I hear Mum rinse the sherry glass in the sink and busy herself at the stove. I hear the driver's door slam shut and the sharp gravel shifting as he walks towards the house. The screen door creaks on its worn hinges and he is here, inside the house. Muted voices from the kitchen and the fridge door opening and the fizz from the beer and the clink of the bottle top spinning on the bright metal of the sink. The weight of him settling into his chair at the head of the table.

Kookaburras laugh in the falling light and crickets drum in the darkening earth.

I wait.

Maybe he'll laugh at the results of my report, pat me on the head and tell me that I need to try harder.

A pig flies past my bedroom window.

I rise from my bed with the bright envelope in my hand and leave the safety of my small room. I stop just outside my bedroom door. My body feels light and distant from me. A thousand steps from the blue-black highway to where I stand. Ten more steps will etch this day into my memory forever. I know it like the certainty of breath. I take the first step and the other nine follow in a blur of time and space till I'm standing before him, already beaten. I offer the envelope.

My mother starts to sob; it's a ploy, a diversion – she hopes that the tears might soften him.

'I failed four subjects!' I say, hoping that the honesty might help.

He slides the pages out and scans them. Pins drop in the quiet.

'Wait in the shed,' he says.

'No, Bruce!' Mum whispers through the tears.

He slams the beer mug on the table, his face already flushing with the anger and the disappointment.

'Get out!' he roars.

I'm already through the screen door and into the yard. I run past the shed and head deep into the dark bush. I'll run away and never come back. I hide deep in the undergrowth with the night things rustling around me.

I hear shouting from the house as Mum pleads with him. More yelling and then the unmistakable sound of a slap and my mother screaming and my blood surging through my heart.

I race back to the house, stopping just outside, where the light doesn't reach. 'Leave her alone! Leave my mother alone, Dad!' I wait there, afraid, but desperate to save Mum.

I know he'll come for me, and he does. If I was only bigger I'd stop this now, but I'm not, I'm only twelve. I wait like a sacrifice. There's no stick in his hand this time; he doesn't need one. It's not about my failure in the exam; it wasn't about my behaviour or even the price of fruit when I was young either. He tells himself that these are the reasons. No, he just wants to hurt me, plain and simple. He wants to feel my young flesh bruise under his fists, he wants to see my blood and feel the terror in me. The first punch splits my bottom lip open, the next one bruises my nose at the bridge and the third one is like the next ten or twenty or pick a random number and you might be close. It must be good to have such an easy target. I don't duck, I don't weave, I stand for as long as I can and let the punches find their chosen marks. One of my eyes is closed already and my pyjamas are torn and shredded from the fury of the attack.

When it was over I got myself to bed somehow. I remember worrying about Mum till the night claimed me. The next morning I was told I could have a week off school. The damage had healed by the time I returned and I told anyone who asked that I had been away with the flu.

Another secret.

INTERMISSION

Fifteen

My father never hit me again. He made the mistake of challenging my brother not long after he had assaulted me. My brother was eighteen at the time. He took the abuse for as long as he could stand it and then knocked my father to the ground with a single, sharp jab to the chin. My brother was banished from the house and was gone by nightfall. He stayed away a year. My father went to bed for a week.

My sister left home the moment she finished high school and was accepted into teachers college in Newcastle. Her time at Stillways was harder even than my brother's or mine; as a girl she was more vulnerable, and the abuse she suffered was relentless, physically and emotionally.

It was the start of the fall. My father had run out of opponents to vent his rage on and his demons were circling in the dark, but that's enough of him now – we can move on. From my father and first loves and ripe tomatoes.

It's 1966 and I'm fifteen now.

I'm taller, without being tall, solid build, blue-eyed.

I am still generous of spirit, though maybe not as much as when I was younger, when I thought that everything was possible and everyone was sane.

Stillways has changed as well. Two years ago, blokes from the electricity company swarmed up the greying poles, strung the thick black cables, and with the flick of a switch, power surged through the old house like new blood and finally woke us. We cleaned the soot from years of gloom and lamplight, and suddenly there was nowhere to hide, now that the shadows had been driven out.

We have appliances. We have whitegoods. We have a Scandinavian-designed lounge that can best be described as modular. There's an oil heater where the open fire used to be and a television where nothing used to be.

I've started to smoke. I don't do it a lot, but when I do I enjoy it a lot. It's the dark sulphurous taste on my tongue and the heat in my lungs and the heady buzz from the first hit that does it for me.

I masturbate a lot. We've got a masturbation club going at school. Chris Dodds is the current champion. The rules of the club are a bit loose and ill-defined, but it basically comes down to who cums first, wins. Doddsie's got his dick in his hand more often than a biro, whenever and wherever the mood takes him, and it takes him a lot, and he doesn't much care who's around at the time. He has no shame. None of us do.

We've been known to sit around in a circle in the bush that borders the school oval. Eight boys under a tall gum tree, beating off. It's just totally weird, given there is nothing vaguely erotic about the drab Australian bush. It would have made a great Tom Roberts painting, *The Wankers at Noon*. Put that in a gilt frame and hang it in the National Gallery in Canberra.

The perfect crime

Eddy Pitt was a rebel. He was small for his age with a shock of bright red hair. He was in my year but not in my class. He couldn't read or write. He spent his time in class drawing pictures of horses in the one exercise book he possessed. He was mad about horses and wanted to be a jockey. He used to wag school on Wyong race days, when he earnt money running errands for bookies. If you ever wanted anything all you had to do was to ask Eddy and he'd get it for you, anything, and if he couldn't get it he generally knew somebody who could. He was a thief, there was no doubt about it.

It was thought that he was responsible for a lot of break-and-enters around town but he had never been caught. He didn't cause any trouble at school, just went quietly about his business and kept pretty much to himself. He used to sell single cigarettes to kids, and although it was common knowledge, he had never been busted and no one had ever dobbed on him. He had a dangerous air about him.

There was a rumour going around that his father was doing life in prison for murder, but like everything else about him it was just a rumour. His mother was a small, severe woman. They lived in a weatherboard cottage on the edge of Wyong River.

Eddy is on his way to school one morning when he sees two large green tree snakes entwined together on a low branch. He catches them both and puts them into his school case along with the one exercise book and the box of contraband fags. His first class that morning is science, so before the class starts he sneaks into the laboratory and leaves the case with the snakes on the teacher's desk with the word *SPECIMENS* written on the top in chalk. (He must have got someone to write it for him because he couldn't spell.)

So the hooter goes off and everyone troops into the lab, including Eddy. Miss Knowles, the teacher, sees the case on her desk and doesn't consider it unusual; kids are always bringing in things from their homes or their gardens, like silk worms and cicadas and the like, and she encourages it.

Eddy's given the case a few decent bangs with a large stick just prior to placing it on the desk, so the big snakes are pissed right off. Miss Knowles marks the roll then pops the latches on the case with a sunny 'What do we have here, I wonder?'

She doesn't have to wonder long because the moment they see daylight the snakes are out and angry. They're not venomous but they do bite and that's exactly what the largest snake does. It slides up the inside of her left arm and sinks its fangs in just below the elbow, continues straight across her chest, over her right shoulder, down her back and slithers to the floor.

The other snake is so freaked out by Miss Knowles's bloodcurdling scream that it bites her on the thumb that is still resting on the latch of the case.

Now all the girls in the class are screaming and half the boys as well. This further alarms the snake that has just bitten her, so it decides to fight on and rears into the classic S-shaped strike position, its mouth wide open and air hissing through its fangs.

The larger snake is still sliding around on the well-polished floor, looking for an escape route. Eddy is helping things along by yelling 'Snake! Snake!' at the top of his lungs. Meanwhile a distraught Miss Knowles, grasping her swollen thumb and attempting to nurse her punctured elbow while avoiding the advancing snake, has stepped back and managed to get one of her shoes wedged inside the metal wastepaper bin beside her desk.

Someone has finally flung the door open and the classroom empties in a heartbeat. The snake on the floor has found the replica human skeleton and is making its way up between two of the leg bones towards the pelvic region. Meanwhile, Miss Knowles, who has just about reached the end of her tether, drives her free foot deep into the wastepaper bin in a last-ditch effort to free herself. The second foot becomes wedged in beside the first and now she is teetering on the too-small base of the bin and has slipped too far away from the desk to support herself. The teeter becomes more of a sway, the sway becomes a lurch, till finally she is in free-fall, knocking herself out on the corner of the desk on the way down.

The scene now resembles something from an Agatha Christie murder mystery. There is a woman lying perfectly still on the polished floor of a science laboratory. A vibrant green snake slides through the ribcage of some human remains.

Eddy makes his way to the front of the room, picks up his battered case from the desk, and rubs out the word *SPECIMENS* with the blackboard eraser. He crosses the quadrangle as the hooter sounds for the start of his next class, woodwork, the only subject he really enjoys.

Miss Knowles survives the ordeal with nothing more than a dull pain in her head and four puncture marks in her skin. No one ever finds out who brought the snakes to school. The only clue is the fact that there was a brown case on her desk when she entered the classroom, so that narrows it down to around eleven hundred suspects. Eddy is a suspect, but he's always a suspect, and without proof it is, as always with him, just another rumour.

Earthbound

I'm on a mission.

I walk from the pilot's briefing room. My flight helmet is heavy in my hand. The jumpsuit hugs my broad shoulders, my blue eyes like pale crystal in the dawn light. A slash of red on the horizon. The sun's first rays glint on the sharp edges of the jet. It's just another day in the defence of our nation. The ground crew busy themselves under the belly of the Mirage. After the walk around I climb the stout ladder and settle myself into the snug cockpit, or what I like to call 'the office'. Main switch and the systems come to life, needles in the green, the preflight done, the turbine whirring through the ignition sequence and the jet engine screaming to life. The attack dog is straining at the leash.

'RAAF Mirage Lima Delta is prepared for takeoff.'

'Roger, Mirage Lima Delta – taxi 36R and hold.'

A short taxi and I hold as a Hercules drops out of the sky to touch and go. I watch him climb and bank to the east through the thin early cloud. I'm cleared to go and rolling.

'Stephen Bisley!' Turbulence!

I'm back in the small classroom at the Royal Australian Air Force recruitment centre in George Street, Sydney. I got the early train from Wyong at five-thirty am to be here by nine. I'm here with ten other hopefuls. We've finished the aptitude test that will determine our suitability for the Air Force. I had a little problem with the maths component of the test, but I'm fairly certain I'm not colourblind, so all up I'm feeling pretty confident. I've got blue eyes that match the uniform. I can almost smell the aviation gas already, and secretly I know I've got what it takes.

'Stephen Bisley?'

'Roger,' I blurt out, my head still in the clouds, and then correct myself with the more conventional, 'Yes?'

There's a bloke in a uniform and overshined shoes with a sheaf of papers and a clipboard. 'Follow me, please!' he snaps.

'Sir!' I reply, like I know the drill.

I follow him down a short beige corridor to a small partitioned office. On one wall is a photo of the Roulettes, the Air Force precision-flying team, in tight formation with the Harbour Bridge behind them. They're flying dangerously close together, just the way us pilots like it: high, fast and deadly. The Queen's on the other wall; she's not going anywhere. He points to a chair and drops into another one. He looks at me for the first time and jots something down on a neat form. I think it could be something about my sky-blue eyes. It could also be about the size of my ears, which are a bit large, but I'm growing into them, though it seems to be taking a while.

'Stephen Bisley. Is that you?'

'Yes, sir, last time I looked!'

He doesn't seem to get the joke. Too much on his mind apparently. Weighty decisions to be made. He writes again.

I imagine it's something like *Takes orders well and responds with clarity.*

I wait; I always seem to be waiting for something. He scribbles on. I look at him closely. He's middle-aged with the first tufts of grey at the temples. Probably sat where I am twenty years ago and didn't make the grade. Must be hard for him, meeting all these future pilots, knowing that his life will be lived out in this office, earthbound, shuffling papers, while the people he met here so briefly soar across the wide canopy of the sky, a mile above where he sits. Must be tough.

'Okay, Stephen. I've just been going through the results of your test and the school reports you brought with you today. Based on the information I have before me, I am pleased to say that we are able to offer you the choice of two positions in our next intake, providing you pass the medical examination. We have vacancies for AFDGs at the moment – would that be something that might interest you?'

AFDG. I run the letters through my head slowly and there's nothing in their line-up that says 'pilot' to me, unless it's the 'F' bit, which could have something to do with flight.

'Air Field Defence Guard,' he explains, seeing the vacant, slightly puzzled look on my face.

The only word that means anything to me in the title is the Air bit; the others sound wrong, especially Field and Guard. There's been a giant mistake or perhaps a simple error.

'I want to be a pilot,' I assert, but my voice sounds thin and reedy.

'A pilot? Stephen, if I had a dollar for every kid who sat where you are now and said they wanted to be a pilot, I'd be a rich man! Let me take you through this: a) We don't take people of your age into flight school; b) You don't possess the necessary educational requirements; and c) I don't give a fuck whether you have blue eyes or not!'

He didn't actually say the last line, but he might as well have.

He continued. 'Do you like animals, Stephen? Because if you did decide to enlist as an Air Field Defence Guard, you might have the opportunity of working with a dog – possibly a German shepherd!'

There was no stopping him now.

'The only other course that would suit your ability would be as a cook, with the possibility of perhaps becoming a chef!'

Seems fitting, because right now I can feel the egg on my face.

'Lima Delta, we have taken heavy enemy fire and will have to abort the mission!'

'Lima Delta, out!'

*

The morning sun is just on the horizon. There's a small sandy mound in the middle of the Woomera Rocket Range. There is nothing but desert out here. It stretches to the horizon on all sides. If you turn in a circle slowly you can see the rim of the earth the entire way around. There is a sound like distant thunder. A sleek Mirage fighter blisters the azure blue sky; its wings cut the dawn light like bright sabres. It levels out at a bare hundred feet above the spinifex on its deadly strafing run. I'm not in the jet. I'm standing on the small sandy mound with my new best friend, Rex.

One of us is watching the jet. One of us has his tail between his legs, and it's not the dog.

I left the Air Force Rejection Centre and threw myself under a passing bus.

Just joking. The city was hot in the early afternoon. The crowds surged along George Street and bunched at the intersections. I was country slow at first and it took me two blocks before I found the rhythm and got into my stride. It was two-thirty pm; I had more than three hours before my train left at six. I let the human tide carry me up George Street towards Central Station. No plan in my head, just happy to be on the move. At Park Street, I stepped out of the stream and headed east towards Hyde Park to take a load off and feel some space around me.

I knew the city layout from earlier trips with my family, not well, but the landmarks were in my head: the harbour to the north, south to Central Station, Hyde Park just east of Elizabeth Street. At the park I circled the fountain and headed south to the quiet of the War Memorial, found a patch of dappled sun and stretched out on the grass. I watched the city for a while. Pea-green double-decker buses whining on the downgrade on William Street with their speed washing off as they climbed to Kings Cross. School kids on an excursion to the squat brown museum on College Street. Lovers entwined on the grass, and further along a homeless man, with everything in a cart, fed stale bread to dusty bobbing pigeons. So much to see here. I rolled onto my back for a break from it and let the blue, blue settle and quieten me.

I was never going to be a pilot. It was just a shot at freedom, a chance to make a start at something; a way out, an exit. I lay with my thoughts for a while, the sun winking through the leafy canopy above me and the sounds of the city rising and falling. I was loosening the ties. My parents knew it, I knew it. I would sit the School Certificate towards the end of the year and that would be it. I didn't know what I would do after school but today was a start.

I shake the park off me and head south for Central Station and the train home. By the time I hit the Haymarket on the edge of Chinatown I know I belong here, in this city. It's the energy of the place. Everyone going somewhere, moving en masse, to get ahead, to be the first, to be a part of it.

I sit in the cafeteria at Central with tea and a corned beef and pickle sandwich. I buy the latest *Phantom* comic from the newsstand. I make my way to the country train platform and board the train to Wyong. I find an empty compartment and settle into the seat beside the window. The sky is darkening as we leave the city and clatter up the northern line. Lights winking on in the houses, kids in the yards in the dusk, a woman at the sink in a bright window, men walking home with rolled papers under their arms and the light from the streetlamps pooling on the footpath.

Out of the city now and through the sandstone walls to cross the Hawkesbury River, the plump oysters sleeping on their wooden beds, the tide washing them clean. Climbing now, an hour to go and I unfurl the comic and lose myself in the inky pages. This one's all about pirates, and by page four he's knocked three guys out and he's working on the fourth. I close the comic with other thoughts in my head. I think I'm done with the Phantom. I think I'm done with a lot of things today.

I sit on the slowing train.

I wish my family had been closer, more loving. I know we were all capable of it, ready for it, wanting it. Dad had put a stop to it. I still don't know why. He'd killed it off in all of us; in Mum, in Richard, in Kristin and in me.

I just wish we had been better.

The train arrives at Wyong and I get the bus for the last leg of the trip. An hour later I'm walking down Carter's Road. The moon is high and bright, the paperbarks shining white in the bush, the bright road ahead and the night things moving. I'm leaving this. A small farm at the end of a dusty road. A place of too many secrets.

Mum gave me a poem the next morning at breakfast:

> What did she do, the old woman in the shoe,
> When all the children left?
> Did she feel bereft?
> Rather she put back seven chops,
> And went less often to the shops.

That's my mum.

Surf's up

I am almost over having sex with myself and would like to include another person. It seems such an appalling waste of resources, and I have so much to give! If there is a god, which I have always doubted, I would like a blonde with large breasts. Someone like Marilyn Monroe, the blonde of all blondes. She died in 1962, when I was eleven. I do know that if we had met, I could have made her happy, if only briefly – seconds, perhaps.

I wouldn't mind brunettes, if it wasn't for the hair.

You put a blonde of ample proportions in a bikini on a beach with a little smudge of zinc across her lightly freckled nose. Apply a thin film of lotion to her body and you're fairly close to heaven. I spend a lot of time at the beach – most weekends. It's not all about the scantily clad girls. I've got an eight-and-a-half-foot Gordon Woods three-stringer mal that I bought off a mate. It's a bit big for me but I can get it to turn if I lie right back on it and really swing my weight through my hips with the nose up. It's a plank.

The beach was the place to be. If I could get a mate with a car to pick me up and help haul the mal onto the racks, then I was gone for the day. We had a few different spots. Catherine Hill Bay was the closest to my place, about five miles north, and a little further was Caves Beach, just before Swansea. Going south, Norah Head had a point that worked if the nor'easter was pumping.

Catherine Hill Bay was like an Australian version of a Welsh mining village. It had a single doglegged main street that cut through the rows of miners' cottages and ran downhill to the coal loader that jutted into the bay.

The loader ran out from the southern end of the beach to the deep blue of the ocean way beyond the breakers, deep enough for the coal-carrying ships to load and go. When the offshore winds blew from the west it shaped the sets into long perfect waves that broke to the left from the northern end and ran the entire length of the bay to the south. It took all the strength I had to get the big board moving fast enough, but if you nailed one the ride was sensational. The board accelerating across the face to the left, the nose chattering under your feet as the speed came on. The wave folding and breaking behind and the fizz of the spray off the crest as the wind pushed the face upwards into a perfect curve with the board slicing through like a blade.

When we weren't in the water we were not far from it. We'd hang out with the local babes on the beach, some we knew, some we wanted to know. There was something about the surf and the sun that mellowed everyone and turned us on. If things heated up too much there was always the privacy of the sand dunes up behind the beach. It was all just innocent fun and the joy of being young.

On days when the surf was really pumping, the guns would arrive, crews from Newcastle and Sydney and beyond – surfers who travelled the coast in search of the action. The word of mouth through the surfing community was incredible. Someone would have heard from someone else that the bay was going off and bang, they'd all be there.

These dudes surfed the world. Bali in Indo, California and the legendary Laniakea in Hawaii, where the waves would thunder in, thirty foot high and deadly.

They'd arrive in panel vans with a dozen boards on the racks or VW Kombis with peace signs and dolphin and whale stickers on the windows. They had the best-looking girls on the coast, chicks that hung with the best of the best. Babes they'd met on the beaches of Bali, South Africa, Hawaii. Exotic chicks with skin as black as local coal, their hair in beaded braids. Athletic blondes from Baja who could ride you off any wave they chose.

These guys had bodies like warriors. Scarred torsos from wipeouts that could kill you. Muscled arms like coiled rope, huge calluses below their knees from years of paddling, the sea through them like blood and their eyes the colour of dreams. We were in total awe of them.

We'd leave the water when these guys showed up. It wasn't an option to stay. They could do things on their boards that just made us look pathetic. So we'd climb to the headland behind the dunes to watch the show and wait to get our beach back.

*

Other days I'd ride my bike out to the bay. Sometimes there'd be people I knew, sometimes there wasn't. I was happy to be there either way, happy to be on my own. Sometimes I preferred it. It was a great place to work things out, to think things through. I'd sit up on the headland and just look. If you looked long enough it became a meditation of sorts, with the flow of the waves, the change of the light on the water, the constant movement across the surface and the awesome energy and power of it. It smelt like ozone and salt. Some days, when the big westerlies blew, the sea became dark and troubled. The currents were a confusion of direction, the backwash met the incoming sets and spoilt them before they broke. Always changing, never constant, never reliable, never safe – never.

I was at the bay one Saturday. Lots of families on the beach, plenty of sun, umbrellas on the sand and kids playing on the shore. A light nor'easter rippling the water. We were just lying around as you do, a few mates and some local girls. Towels in the circle, talking and snoozing as the mood took us. Then someone shouting and people pointing, a crowd gathering, bronzed bodies surging through the waves and more heading out through the break line. Panic on the beach. 'Is it a shark?'

'No! Someone's in trouble out the back, there where the board riders are – look, there, see?'

Red and yellow caps arriving fast and more confusion, more bodies diving deep, bronzed feet kick the air at the surface, down and back for air and down again and further down. A sinking man lifted from the clammy deep. A body brought to shore, as still as a churchyard.

'He's Japanese,' says someone in the circling crowd.

'They're not used to the water, not great swimmers.' That's Merle from the fish shop, who knows everything and more. The lifesavers blow the giving breath into him and pump him for an hour, but he was dead before they found him, floating in the land of shadows. They found his towel after everyone had gone home. At least they presumed it was his. It was the last one on the beach and no one could understand the weird writing on the label, and the neat thongs were different from the local ones.

*

Just south of Catherine Hill Bay was another beach called Frazer Park, north of a rocky outcrop called Snapper Point. I was only six years old and my sister was nine. Dad had taken us for a swim on a mild Sunday morning in early summer. Dad was a keen body surfer and had taught us all to surf.

I was fooling around in the shallows and making crude sandcastles on the beach. Dad had taken Kris out to the surf line and they were catching waves in the moderate swell. There was no one else on the beach. Unbeknown to my father, a rip had formed as the outflow had broken through the sandbar and large volumes of water were surging through the break and pouring out to sea. Kris had caught a wave to the beach and was heading back out to where my father was waiting. I remember looking up and seeing my sister being drawn out to sea, locked in the power of the current in the rip. I could see the look of terror on her face as it swept her further and further from the shore.

She was panicking now and trying to swim against it back to the safety of the beach, one small girl against the power of the sea. The swell was increasing in size and she had now reached the surf line, and the big waves were collapsing on her and driving her down. I saw my father swimming madly through the turbulence to get to her. By the time he reached her, they were right in the strike zone, pummelled by each breaking wave.

Dad managed to get them both within thirty yards of the shore and my sister was able to surf a broken wave to the beach. Dad had used up so much energy in the rescue that he was now being drawn out himself and was weakening by the second. I will never forget how vulnerable and helpless he looked as he was swept further and further away from us.

Then there was the blur of a body beside us and a young surfer hurled himself into the water, settled himself on his board and surged out through the breakers. By now all we could see from the beach was the dot of my father's black hair far beyond the swell. He must have been close to letting go when the surfer reached him. He hauled Dad onto his board and they sat out there waiting for a break in the swell, then the surfer brought our father back to the shore and to us and to life. I remember Dad collapsing on the sweet sand till the fear had left him.

We drove home slowly, the smell of the sea still in the car, damp towels on the seat, all of us caught by what might have been. That night my father's life runs through him like sand, and he counts every breath till dawn.

In another bedroom, I lay awake and imagined life without him.

Frazer Park was treacherous, but so was every beach, on the wrong day. Snapper Point had a rock ledge that jutted out from the bottom of the cliff face into the sea. It was a haven for rock fishermen. On a good day the sea sat a good nine feet below the ledge. On a bad day it was anyone's guess and you were a fool to trust it, but there's plenty of fools out there.

They'd arrive with their buckets and rods and boxes of hooks, jigs, lures, sinkers, prawns, pilchards, weed and squid. Weatherproof windcheaters and a box of beer and a mate. You might luck out and get a feed; you might go home with nothing – it's all part of the game. Every now and then something dark would stir way out in the deep blue, something would shift, a different thing. A current that met another current that wasn't usually there. Wind shear off a distant cliff face that stalled one wave as it formed and drove it deep into the one behind, a cross current, a fluke, a freak, call it what you will. Out of nowhere, out of a calm blue sea it would come, a blue-green monster of a thing.

When it hit it detonated like a bomb, the rock shelf blasted clean of everything. Two men in the dark water, the beer cans bobbing like bright beacons, the morning's catch, an hour dead now, floating on the surface like real fish do. The busted men, face down in the water, float like real men don't. Big things listening from the deep. Dark shapes circling, spiralling up and up. A nudge first, followed by another, looking for signs of life, then bigger things coming, rising from the gloom to look. A nip, just to make sure. Then the first bite, blood in the water and all hell breaks loose, small slithering things strike like arrows between the sharks that rip and tear and gnaw and gorge. The marrow from the split bones floating through the strewn current. Torn hair drifting in the swell as small things suck the follicles loose.

Then the sea calm and quiet again.

The wave gone like a bleak memory.

Peaches

I spend as much time away from home as I can these days. Weekends I have a job picking peaches and nectarines in the Carters' orchard. I love the work. Climbing the tall ladders in the avenues of trees. Feeling the soft furry skin of the delicate fruit nestled in my hand. Freeing them with a slight twist. The weight of the calico bag growing heavier as we strip the laden branches. Emptying them into the bins in the trailer behind the tractor. Tea from a thermos at mid-morning and then back to work again till lunch. Looking behind me down the rows with the plucked trees shimmering. Only four till the end now and the race to finish and a sense of achieving something worthwhile. My body tired from the effort of good work. Dollars in my pocket on the way home, a bath from heaven, and sleep, warm and deep.

Back again on Sunday, the ladder against the first tree of a new row, the peaches dewy to the touch before the orchard warms and the fruit comes easy to the hand. Talking and laughing between the trees, racing for fun, fruit fights with the rotten ones, sorting in the packing shed and Sunday slipping through our sticky fingers and the stripped orchard darkening in the dusk.

When the fruit was finished I got a job at the local fitness camp. It was run by the education department, the people who brought you warm milk and free ink. There was one on the southern end of Lake Macquarie, only a bike ride from home. My scoutmaster, Mike Collins, worked there and he got me a job in the kitchen. The head chef was an old poof and used to try to feel me up in the coolroom. I'd be in there struggling with boxes of produce when these meaty hands would encircle me. I started carrying a knife in my work boot. We fed two hundred hungry kids three meals a day for two weeks. Five hundred eggs at breakfast, mounds of bacon, tubs of baked beans, cereal for days and gallons of milk.

When they weren't being fed, the kids were in canoes on the lake or on the archery range or doing gymnastics in the sports hall. At night they'd twist sticky dough around green sticks like I used to do when I was twelve and cook the damper over the campfire. The teachers would lead them in songs like 'Ging Gang Goolie Goolie Wash Wash' and 'Youth is Calling', rousing songs guaranteed to make you fit just by singing them. Ghost stories around the dying fire, and more songs and quizzes and stories and talent quests. Sometimes I'd stay late and join them around the fire. Young faces golden in the firelight, the wonder still in them, secure, safe and happy.

I still worked around the farm. There was always something to do. Fences to mend, a bit of ploughing, always something. It wasn't producing anything anymore. Not that it ever did really, but Dad liked to think he was a farmer. He's not drowning cats anymore; we've run out of them. We ate the last of the chooks and the horses have gone to greener pastures. He spends a fair amount of time in his new recliner in the lounge room. He likes it that much he's spending less time in his other place at the head of the table. Anyway, there's nothing much left to be head of – everyone's gone except Mum and me and one cow in the paddock.

So there he is, horizontal in front of the cricket, a longneck within reach, praying it won't rain so he can stay in front of the telly for a full five days. He's still teaching others the things he can't teach us.

He's on auto a bit these days. I've never seen him teach. Never had the chance. He never let any of us attend a school where he was teaching. I always thought it was an ethical decision and believed that for years. Now I'm not so sure. Without us there, he had absolute freedom to do whatever it was he didn't want us to see. More secrets.

A view from the bridge

I'm in Robbie Ihlein's car and we're nicking off from school at lunchtime. It's another market day and it's raining so the whole thing's been a washout. I'm in the front seat with Robbie; Gary Attenborough and Dicky Dunn are in the back. We're going to The Entrance, just to hang around and see what's happening. Sometimes something does. Sometimes nothing does. Today it happens! It happens big time!

We're driving to Gosford over The Entrance bridge. The rain is falling in grey sheets, the sky is low and heavy. We check out a couple of beaches on the way, but there's no one around because of the rain, so the plan is to get to The Entrance and hang till it clears. No one's talking much in the car. Rain can do that to you. It has a way of dulling people into a state of quiet reflection. So we're just cruising, the muted sound of rain on the roof, wipers on the windscreen, the swish of tyres on the wet road.

'Fuck, check this out! Pull over, Robbie – pull over now!'

Confusion in the car. 'What? What's the matter?' asks Robbie, the car slowing and the rest of us suddenly alert, but not knowing why.

'Pull over now!' Gary's already got the door open, the car's stopping in a no-stopping place, horns blaring from behind, cars swerving in the wet to avoid other cars swerving in the wet. Us all out now, the rain pelting us and Gary at the railing that spans the bridge, pointing down into the deep grey.

Now we all see it through the rain, down in the grey speckled water. We're at the very top of the crest of the bridge, but even at this height, with the rain in our eyes, we see the thing down there in the water. In the centre of the channel that funnels the water under the bridge is a small boat. It's leaning heavily to one side, straining against the anchor rope that slants down into the water from the bow. There is a man in a sodden grey suit and tie in the boat. The top part of his body from the waist up is underwater.

He is lying on his back with his arms outstretched like some floating crucifix, his head fully submerged. His hips are balanced on the side of the boat and one of his feet is caught under the single seat, his body rising and falling in the current. We dive back into the car and Robbie guns it off the bridge, hangs a sharp left at the bottom that leads to a boat hire place on the edge of the water. We bang on the door but the joint's closed because of the weather. The hire boats are bobbing beside the bleached jetty, all chained up and padlocked. We find one untethered beside the workshop; there's a crack in the side of the hull, it's being readied for repair, the wood freshly sanded.

    We lower it off the jetty and get in. There're no oars so we all paddle madly by hand, two a side to even the strokes, the water seeping in through the cracked hull. The stricken boat's three hundred feet away and we're paddling by hand against the tide and the driving rain. We're soaked to the skin from the rain and the waves breaking over the bow. Finally we make it to the stern of the tilting boat and Robbie latches on to it to stop us from drifting away. At first nobody moves. Nobody wants to.

None of us is prepared for what we're about to see.

Finally Gary hauls himself over the high side of the leaning boat. The weight of him causes the boat to right itself and the effect is catastrophic. The top part of the sinking man rears up like some watery phantom, arms outstretched, and collapses face down onto the floor of the boat. The weight of him causes the leg that is trapped under the seat to snap and poke out of the side of what now looks like a sodden bundle of a man.

We leave him where he is, pull the anchor up and use his oars to row us all to shore, the death boat trailing in our wake.

By the time we get back a small crowd has gathered on the jetty at the boat hire place. People crossing the bridge had seen the recovery; there's nothing like a death to draw a crowd. Someone's called the cops, so we tie the boat front and back to the jetty and wait. Sudden celebrities, we wait in an awkward huddle in the rain; it doesn't matter now. Someone's got fags and somehow we get them lit in the wet. The gawkers don't come near us. They just watch and wait for something to happen, something else. The cop arrives in his own car; apparently they're short-staffed or the sarge has gone home early with the squad car or whatever – I'm not really listening. He takes our names and asks us what happened. He scrawls it all in his official notebook. He's probably wondering why we're not at school but he lets it slide, under the circumstances.

I want to ask him why he thinks the guy was in a boat in a suit and tie on a shit-awful day like this, but I let it slide as well, under the circumstances. After a quick look at the dead man, he gets some bigger blokes in the crowd to help him bag up the body and lug it to the car park. They put the body in the boot, on top of the spare tyre, and it takes three goes to get the lid closed; it's something to do with the bloating. I didn't see it but the copper reckons the prawns had eaten the eyes out of his skull and something bigger had removed an ear.

Afterwards, we were worried that we might be sprung by the school, since we'd given the copper our names, but nothing ever came of it. The following week the local newspaper covered the incident on page six, just before the greyhound racing results. It said there had been an accidental drowning and a man's body had been recovered from The Entrance Channel. The police stated there had been 'no suspicious circumstances'.

I agreed, apart from the suit, the tie and the rain.

Trapped

Back at school the talk's all about leaving. Who is, who isn't. There are guys in my class talking about apprenticeships down the mines or at the power station. To call Lake Munmorah home for life. To marry here and every night stare across the lake at the winking power station, or spend your days a mile underground chipping away at the coalface. Another rusting boat in another carport. Your childhood sweetheart feeding the baby in the highchair. Saturday morning you're too crook to get off the lounge because you drank the housekeeping money last night in the pub with your mates who you've known since birth. The baby's crying, your wife's twenty-two and sick of you already. She doesn't know what she wants and she probably never will but she knows she doesn't want you – that's the only thing she's certain of. Your old man in another grey fibro house in the next street. His wife doesn't love him either, she hasn't for forty years, but it's too late to go, for everyone. You've got everything you ever wanted, because you've never wanted anything.

I'm not saying this life is wrong. I'm not saying it was all like that. But there was enough of it that was, and it frightened the hell out of me.

The Brothers Grim

'Come out here, you weak bastard!'

I'm standing in the middle of the yard between the house and the shed. It's Saturday morning and Mum and Dad have gone shopping to Newcastle and won't be home for hours. Good thing, because I'm going to kill my older brother. I'm going to murder him.

I'm going to dump his body in the creek, but not until I've tortured him with fire and electricity and petrol and a stock whip. I haven't got the other stuff, but I've got the whip, coiled and stuck down the back of my pants so it can't be seen from the front.

'You wear a bra and panties and everyone knows you're a girl!' I yell, trying to prise him from the house. Nothing stirs. I know he's in there. He came into my bedroom earlier and ripped up two of my comics, then punched me really hard on the top of my arm. He says he knows that I've taken one of his girlie magazines and if I don't give it back in ten minutes, he's going to tie me to a bull ants' nest and put honey on my balls.

That's when I went to the shed and got the whip. I'm really good with a stock whip; I practise a lot. I put small bits of paper on the lawn and crack them with the lash. I never miss. I got my cousin Peter, who lives across the creek, to hold some paper in his mouth. He was so brave and you can hardly notice the scar.

'Dick Bisley is a dickhead!' I yell. 'Come out here and I'll punch your lights out, you knob!'

The screen door opens and he's on the verandah, looking really pissed off. Good!

'What did you say?'

'I said you're a fuckwit!' I feel the stock whip coiled against my back; all he needs is a little shove and he's mine.

'Chick, chick, chicken,' I yell across the yard.

'Give me my magazine back, you little bastard,' he roars, 'or I'll knock you out.' He's getting really worked up now; he's taken the bait.

'Oh, I'm soooo scared … look, I'm shaking in my boots!'

I shake. That does it. He leaps off the verandah and starts towards me, a murderous look in his eyes.

I reach behind my back and the whip's in my hand in an instant, uncoiling and vicious. He sees it and stops dead in his tracks, the venom draining from his face. I smile. Now he's in no-man's land. I flick the whip behind me in preparation for the strike.

He can't go forward, he can't go back, he's caught like the low mangy dog he is. My left arm is still throbbing from where he punched me but I'm about to even the score. He has two choices here: he can charge me head-on in the hope that he can get inside the whip before the lash gets him, or he can try and outrun it. I don't like his chances either way. I flick the lash back and forth a few times to help him make up his mind.

'Not so tough now, are you?' I taunt. 'Picking on a sixteen-year-old when you're twenty-one!' His eyes dart around and I know he's about to move. My right arm tenses, my hand tightens on the handle of the whip. He spins to the left and sidesteps right, hoping I'll be fooled by the move. He's only covered a few feet when I bring the whip forward in a whistling arc. My arm loops around my head, the whip now at full extension, then I drop my elbow and flick my wrist at the same time. The thin plaited leather snakes through the air like a scythe, the lash at the very tip turns ballistic, hurtling towards the target at Mach speed. He's only ten feet away when the lash finds its mark. I draw the whip back behind me in case he comes again, but I needn't have bothered. For the moment he seems to have forgotten about me. He seems more concerned with a small area on the right cheek of his arse, like it's suddenly caught fire. His legs are dancing in an apparent attempt to outrun the burning sensation and he has just screamed like a girl at a Beatles concert. Now he heads off towards the house clutching his bum. He disappears into the laundry and I hear the sound of water running and I guess he's dousing the flames.

Then he's back, heading across the verandah, water dripping from the back of his pants and a broom in his hands. A broom? I hadn't really planned for this. The murderous look is back on his face and he's coming, fast.

I circle the whip around my head and crack the lash as a warning, but all it seems to do is make him madder. I unleash the whip again in a last attempt to dissuade him. Same action as before, arm, wrist, the sound of the thin leather whistling, the lash seeking the target. At the very last moment he lifts the broom handle above his head and the leather wraps around it like a snake on a stick. With one swift action he wrenches the whip from my hand. Something thin loosens in my bowels.

I am standing in front of a bullet-ridden whitewashed wall in some lawless Mexican town. My bloodstained shirt is open to my waist. I am blindfolded; my arms are tied behind my back. I know in my troubled heart that I have fought hard for the revolution, but it's come to this. I hear the sound of the rifles being cocked, I feel the wild adrenalin in my chest, the last breath ragged in my throat. I wait, and wait, and finally it comes with a … BANG!

The punch isn't hard but it is enough. A light flickers somewhere far, far away, trees whirl in circles above my head, and my hand reaches for something that isn't there. I don't think I am out for long, maybe seconds, but my jaw aches and my ears are ringing. I sit on the grass for a while till the fog lifts.

I think the whole thing has gone rather well, apart from the end bit. One all, till next time. I head off to the house for a bit of a lie-down before the folks get home. I don't know where my brother is and I don't care. I stretch out on my bed. I'm already planning the next ambush; maybe next time I'll bring a whip *and* a gun! I slide the girlie magazine out from under my pillow. I flick it open and you know something? The blonde on page two is almost worth the headache.

Prizes

A month before we're due to sit our School Certificate, we have the annual prize-giving day at school. It is held at the Wyong picture theatre, scene of many of my crimes, the most memorable being my disastrous attempt at a first date with Barbara Dunstan. (I am eternally grateful that she never told a soul what happened on that awful night.)

It's a Friday and the entire school population is in the theatre, over a thousand of us, plus the teaching staff and the office people and the mothers who run the school canteen and the groundsmen. On stage is the official party, comprising the masters of each teaching department, the headmaster and the deputy head, and the school captains, with the remaining teaching staff seated on either side.

Finally the crowd settles as the Goog walks to centre stage. For this auspicious occasion the school crest is displayed proudly on the front of the lectern, with the motto *Tentando Superabis* emblazoned across it. I had written it above the urinals in the boys' toilets at school, because at last I'd discovered that translated from the Latin it means 'Aim High'. To this day I still think that was a stroke of genius. The Goog leads off with one of his stock openers along the lines of 'what a great year it's been for the school'. He wishes the fourth form students success in our upcoming exams and counsels us about using the next month's study time wisely, as opposed to surfing most days, sneaking into pubs, hitting on chicks and generally goofing off, which most of us are intending to do. Warm applause ensues. Now the boring bit begins, the awards ceremony. We start with achievements in sport.

I've seen the running order. There's about three million golden trophies lined up on several tables beside the stage and it's going to take roughly a week and a half to get through them, and that's before we even get to the egghead awards. I sink low in my seat. I'm bored already.

Up they come, one after another, the fit people! The swimmers are first, all those poor bastards who have been getting up before dawn from the moment they were born to swim up and down a bit of blue water.

I remember my first swimming lesson, when I was four. The instructor threw me into the deep end to see how I went. I went straight to the bottom and had to be rescued, coughing and spluttering. It took me years to get my confidence back.

The divers come next. I admire them. They have courage. I tried going off the top of the diving tower at the Wyong pool. I couldn't do it. I looked down at the small patch of blue and had to retreat back down the ladder. I get vertigo in Cuban heels!

On and on it goes, award after award. Finally the last high-jumper leaves the stage and we break for lunch, only to return an hour later for more of the same. Now it's the academics' turn. It's a geek fest. Up they come one after the other, the pale, bespectacled ones. I don't dislike them; I just think it's unnatural to be that focused. In my opinion, if you're the dux of the school that's a sign you should get out more. Ah, who am I kidding? I'm just jealous really.

We finally get to the end of the academic awards and the deputy headmaster steps up to the microphone. He is going to announce the final award of the day – huge cheer – the Principal's Prize for School Service. He coughs lightly into the microphone, to prepare us all for the weighty words to follow. He raves on about the school being like a family and that a school is only as good as each person in it and that the strength of a family is dependent on each member of it (can't be talking about mine). He talks about the commitment that the recipient of the award possesses and the tireless unrewarded work the person has done and continues to do, blah, blah, blah.

At last he gets there: 'The 1966 Principal's Prize for School Service goes to ... Stephen Bisley of 4B.'

I remember the sea of faces turning towards me. I remember being totally shocked. I don't remember how I got from the back of that dusty old theatre, down the stairs and along the aisle to the stage. I remember Mr Egger standing by the lectern, his hand thrust out before him, and the feeling of his hand gripping mine. The teachers are all on their feet clapping and somebody gives me the largest trophy of the day. The sporting heroes are applauding and the geeks are too, and everyone upstairs stands, causing a ripple like a Mexican wave. People are whistling and somebody yells, 'Good on ya, Bizo!' I do remember standing in the pool of bright light in a theatre looking out at a sea of smiling faces. I do remember when I first arrived at high school thinking that I needed to find my niche, my place, the thing that would give me purpose, and today I think I've found it.

Kristin

'Krissie's coming home on Saturday!'

That's Mum, happy as Larry. Or in her case, as happy as Pauline!

Dad leaves early on Saturday to pick you up from the railway. I can imagine the conversation when you meet at the car.

'Why do you have to wear black all the time? Anyone would think you were in mourning.'

Little does he know you had a joint before you got on the train in Newcastle and there are two more rolled and ready in the pocket of your duffel coat for when it gets too hard at home. It's already too hard and you've only just got off the train. He'll challenge you at least three times before you get to the farm; he thinks it's the only way you'll know him. You sit quietly in your own private fog.

There's a kettle on the stove as soon as Mum hears the car; it's for you, this good stout black tea. She's gone to the trouble of warming the pot, because it's you. I'll be waiting on the verandah for you, and I'll make you laugh as soon as I can. You bring the world with you when you come, Krissie. You in the black duffel coat and liquorice-lolly legs. There's cake for Mum and treats from town and something small for Dad.

Your hair is ironed flat to look like Marianne Faithfull. Sometimes you bring recent canvases you've done with the oil paint still sticky. I know you've got boyfriends, but I'll always be here for you. Sometimes you bring girlfriends with you, like Flora with the beautiful open face and the broad smile and a duffel coat too. You both could be from Carnaby Street in Swinging London and go to parties with the Beatles. 'Hey there, Georgy girl.'

Mum claims you at the threshold of the house. The old man fades to the fridge for a beer; it's early, but who's counting? I hover nearby, happy to be close.

We walk in the paddocks in the afternoon with Mum. Dad's not with us; he never is. He sits in his place at the head of the table and hopes you'll notice, but you're way too smart to fall for that one. In the paddocks we're nearly like a family, going nowhere, moving together. We make our way to the creek and sit on the bank under the sighing casuarinas. The sky is in the water today. We swam here when we were small, you and me, where the clay oozed out, just over there, and we caked it in our hair and smeared it over each other and slid through it to the water and washed ourselves clean.

Do you remember running through the low scrub, between the river gums, forgetting that the snakes were there, coiled on the dark ground, to find the riotous Christmas bells waiting to be picked for home?

Mum reminds you of the picnics with the plastic tea set and your dolls arranged around you.

Mum's having a bit of a weep at the memory and we all go quiet till she honks into the hanky that's always folded into one of her sleeves.

You cheer her up with stories from your new life. Cheap Asian restaurants you go to, teachers college, protests you've been to about Vietnam and the bombing of Cambodia and boyfriends with no money and painting classes with nude men on chairs and then: 'When are you going to leave Dad and have a life of your own, Mum?'

More hanky work and then she's up on her feet and moving. 'Enough of that. Let's head back for afternoon tea – Dad'll be ready for a cuppa.' And she's off. We catch her in the paddock and you light another joint and offer it to her.

'I don't know what all the fuss is about with this marijuana thing,' she says, and inhales deeply to prove her point.

Oh dear, this is going to get messy. It doesn't take long for the gear to hit the spot and in no time she's dancing through the clover, stories tumbling out of her along with jokes and bits of songs. Now she's over there cuddling the cow, who doesn't seem to mind but probably thinks it's out of character. We steer her towards the house. Dad's retreated to the lounge room with the next beer and is dozing in the recliner with something blokey on the box.

Mum's now charging round the kitchen like a woman possessed and finally manages to get some tea into the cups.

I'm worried about the boiling water, but she won't let me help, though she needs a hand to find the sugar. I've just seen her put it in the fridge, so I retrieve it and get the milk out while I'm there. Mum's hacking into the cake Kris has brought with the bread knife. I'm more worried about the knife than I was about the water and try to intervene, but she refuses my help and hacks on.

By the time she gets the cake to the table, she's eaten half of it and the remaining pieces look like they've been put through a paper shredder. She finally gets into a chair, has two sips of tea and announces she needs to lie down. It takes her a couple of goes to find the bedroom, and when she gets there she crashes face down on the bed.

This is my family. My father's pissed in the lounge room, my mother's stoned in the bedroom and my sister's ripped in the kitchen. I think I'll make myself a double-strength raspberry cordial just so I feel like I belong.

Sunday afternoon and you're back in the black and ready to go. Only a short ride to the station with Dad now, and then you're free. He's polite on the trip, knowing that he's lost you and wishing he hadn't. Mum's in the kitchen holding the last of the cake you brought in her hands, the salty tears falling to wet the brandied fruit.

On the black ribbon of road that goes all the way to Queensland, Dad drives home to Stillways in an empty car.

Testing times

I took the advice of Mr Egger, the headmaster, and spent the entire month in the lead-up to the exam with my head in a book. Well, a magazine, actually. It was a copy of *Playboy*, a collector's edition, and it was crammed full of information about human anatomy and important advice about stress relief and interesting articles designed to keep the reader abreast of world events.

I'm kidding, sort of. I did work, most days, on some subjects, but it all seemed a bit pointless, a bit late. I took my books to the beach, hoping that the effect of the sun, the sea and the waves might focus me. It did, on the sun and the sea and the waves, but not a lot on the differences between Monet and Manet and what drove Van Gogh to remove an ear. I think a Prussian may have started the First World War by shooting someone important – or was it caused by someone important shooting a Prussian? Note to self: check Prussians and war. Other note to self: check difference between Monet and others.

Finally the big day came: the start of the exams. My first was maths and the only reason I turned up was because it was compulsory. It was scheduled to go for two hours and I completed the paper with an hour to spare, due mainly to the fact that I answered fewer than half the questions. I entertained myself in the remaining time by drawing pictures in the spaces left for the answers. I thought the least I could do was provide some entertainment for the person marking my paper. It was safe to assume that I would not be pursuing a career in accountancy.

The following day was science and, although it wasn't one of my favourites, I enjoyed the test and felt reasonably confident that I had done the best I could.

I had a day's break between science and art history. I had already submitted my major work in art, a study of two ballerinas painted in acrylics. I had wanted to paint a picture of two nudes in a bath, but we didn't have a bath at home and I didn't know two girls who were prepared to pose nude for me, although it wasn't for lack of asking. I had always loved the work of Edgar Degas, who had painted many studies of ballerinas. I loved the movement in his work and the lightness he was able to capture. I don't think my painting was in any way comparable but it was my way of honouring his memory and I was pleased with it.

So on and on it went for the next two weeks. I did get a question in the history exam asking: *What were the events which led to the Outbreak of War in Europe at the end of July, 1914?* Thanks to a bit of last-minute swotting I was able to respond: *The assassination of Archduke Franz Ferdinand, heir to the Austro-Hungarian throne, on 28th June 1914, set in train a series of diplomatic events that led inexorably to the outbreak of the First World War.* So much for the Prussians!

Then, after my last exam, geography, it was all over. Finished.

I remember milling about outside the school hall where the exams had been held with a lot of other kids who, like me, were leaving this year. Everyone seemed numbed by the finality of the day. Eleven years of our lives had been taken up at school. Now the world waited to see what we were worth.

The formal

A week after our exams and I'm in Brooksey's car heading back to school for the last time ever. It's the night of our end-of-year formal. Micky Fisher's in the back seat and we're picking up someone else on the way. I hope it's not Doddsie, the serial wanker; I'm a bit over all that now – I've given it up while I've still got my eyesight.

We look like three FBI agents in our dark suits and, although I can't vouch for myself, I think the others look cool and suddenly older. My suit's a hand-me-down from a cousin who works at the post office. Mum's had to take the pants in a bit and the jacket's a bit long in the sleeves, but it makes me feel capable, like I could be depended on in a crisis, something life-threatening, something urgent and dire.

Mum got a bit emotional when the guys arrived to pick me up. She's quick to cry at the best of times, so it could be anything that set her off. Dad was on his best behaviour, which is a long way from his worst behaviour and didn't even tell me what time to be home. He said, 'Take care,' and went quiet. Mum couldn't help herself and straightened everyone's tie again and had another weep, so we headed off before she got too gushy.

We're on the highway, desperate and dateless and heading south, three G-Men on a mission.

'Have a crack at this,' says Fish from the back, and passes a bottle of Scotch over the seat.

'Started early, did ya?' asks Brooksey, seeing it's already half empty.

'Nah', says Fish, 'it's the old man's. He won't miss it.'

He's probably right. Fish lives in a rundown joint in Wyong with his father. His old man is a notorious drunk; he's been barred from every pub in town. He's not an angry drunk, just an opinionated one, and will argue till the cows come home, so they kick him out every now and then just for a bit of peace and quiet. I don't think I've ever seen him sober and I don't think he's ever had a job. Fish played footy with the Munmorah Red Devils for a while and we'd often go round to his joint early on a Saturday morning to pick him up for the game. He'd always be waiting out the front of his house for us, sitting on the kerb. He didn't ever want anyone to see inside his house, because of the state of it.

His mum had left years ago, just couldn't take it anymore. No one blamed her; she'd just had enough. Fish didn't have a choice, he was only eight when she left and he's been looking after his dad, or trying to, ever since. He has a paper round before school and he works in the local pharmacy on Saturday mornings, delivering prescriptions to old people who aren't mobile. With the money he's able to scrape together and whatever his old man gets from welfare and doesn't drink away, they're able to survive.

The welfare department took Fish away from his dad soon after his mum left and put him in foster care, but Fish was having none of it and ran away from everywhere he was placed and went back home to his dad. He ran away so many times that in the end they just gave up and let him stay at home. The truly amazing thing is that in all the time I've known him, I've never heard him say a bad thing about his dad, not once. He is always neat and tidy at school, is one of the brightest students in the place, and he's funny to boot.

I'd seen his old man in the Royal Hotel, one Saturday morning when I went in there looking for a mate who had a job picking up glasses. Fish's old man had a special place at the end of the bar next to the door to the men's toilet so he didn't have far to go when the urge took him and it took him often. I had heard about his daily drinking routine from Fish, who used to talk about it like it was completely normal and this day I got to see a little of it first hand.

He would be waiting on the footpath for the pub to open at ten. His skin was the colour of pale silk with the tracks of blue veins running just below the surface. His face was ashen and his eyes were sunken and cloudy.

Fish used to try and get some food into him before he left for school in the mornings but he hardly ate, ever.

The moment the pub doors opened, he was in and perched on his bar stool by two minutes past; you could set your watch by him. The barman would have the first white wine of the day poured, with a drinking straw already in the glass. In the mornings Fish's old man shook so violently he couldn't hold the glass. So the barman would hold the straw for him while he drank. It took six glasses for the tremors to settle to the point where he could hold the glass unassisted and then he was set for the day. He sat there all day arguing with anyone who was silly enough to challenge him. He was a font of knowledge from sport to politics and what he didn't know he'd make up, just to prolong whatever discussion he was having at the time. The only time he got off the stool was to relieve himself.

The pub closed at ten, and every night, except Sunday, Fish would be waiting out the front on the footpath, to steer his father home, get his shoes off and get him to bed. In those days pubs were closed on Sundays so Fish's old man drank at home on a barstool Fish had found at the tip and brought home for him. He'd start at ten and drink till ten, seven days a week, three hundred and sixty five days a year. It was like watching a slow suicide. Little did I know.

*

Back in the car, Fish's old man's Scotch gets passed around. I don't go hard on it; it's going to be a long night.

'Who we picking up?' asks Fish.

'You'll see!' says Brooksey as he swings the car off the highway into one of the new estates next to the golf course north of the town.

'Who lives down here, fuckhead?' I ask.

'Jesus Christ, you blokes are like a couple of old sheilas. "Who are we picking up?" "Who lives down here?" Just wait and see!'

We drive down streets lined with the skeletons of new houses under construction. Brooksey turns into a street where the houses are completed, with cars in the driveways and lights in the windows. We stop in front of a blond-brick house with rolls of fresh turf stacked beside the garage. Brooksey kills the headlights.

'Jump in the back, will ya, Bizo?' and he's out the door and moving.

'Yeah, sure,' I say to no one, puzzled. I get in the back seat with Fish and try to hold his hand.

'Fuck off!' he says, and has another belt of the Scotch.

'You better go easy there, tiger, or your old man'll be helping you home for a change,' I say. 'Who's gunna get him from the pub while you're at the dance, or are you just gunna leave him there till tomorrow?' I laugh, so does Fish.

'No, dickhead. I had a word to the publican today, and they're gunna bring him back and dump him in the hammock on the front verandah. I left a blanket for him before I came out. They should bring him home every night, given the amount of money he's dropped on them over the years. Reckon he just about owns the pub by now.'

Brooksey's in the house now; I can see him talking to someone through the open front door.

'What's he doing in there? All the good-looking sheilas will be taken by the time we get to the formal,' says Fish.

Then he's coming down the drive and he's got a girl with him but I can't make out who it is.

'Sly dog!' whispers Fish as they get close to the car. The front doors open together and the interior light blinks on as they both slide in. Brooksey turns to face us.

'This is Susan Green; Sue this is Bizo and Fish. You

remember Sue from primary school, don't ya, Bizo? She was in our class.'

She turns and in a heartbeat I'm in love with her again.

She's just as I remember her. The deep blue of her eyes, the fine nose and the full mouth with the dimples when she smiles. The only difference is she's more beautiful than I remember, absolutely soul-destroyingly, ravishingly beautiful.

'Yeah, hi. How's it going?' I haven't got a thought in my head and I'm surprised that my mouth is working.

'I'm fine, thank you. It's good to see you!'

Fish offers her the Scotch and she declines it with a smile. The doors close and thankfully the inside of the car goes dark. I finally remember to breathe as Brooksey points us to the highway. I can't speak. I haven't seen her in four years but it feels like a lifetime. This is *the* Susan Green, the most beautiful girl in primary school. My first love. The girl I should have taken to the final dance back then and now, four years later, I'm at another final dance and again she's with someone else. This is the Central Coast version of *Romeo and Juliet*, two star-crossed lovers destined never to be together. There's never an apothecary around when you need one.

I feel like I'm on the edge of some kind of madness. I reach for Fish's Scotch in the dark and gulp the liquor down. This is the girl it took me a year to get over and now I'm back in the sadness of first losing her. I know it was young love, but it hurt like hell, it really hurt, and it still does.

'You living back here now?' asks Fish from the dark.

'No, we moved to Sydney when I left primary school. I'm just back visiting my aunty, and Wayne asked me to the formal.'

I want to throw myself out of the car and under a passing truck.

We're suddenly in the glare of the lights of the car park behind the school hall and I don't want to be here.

'Listen, I have to go and make sure the band's got everything they need, so I'll see you in there,' and I'm out of the car and gone. Running away, always running away. I run past the hall and veer down the embankment to the level surface of the back oval, the white sticks of the far goalposts like bright sentinels in the gloom. I make for the tree line and go deep into the bush under the canopy of the looming gums. Then I cry. I cry about Susan, just to get myself going. I cry about leaving home. I cry about my broken family, about the end of things and the beginnings of other things, and when I run out of things to cry about I dig deep and find still more things till I am empty and dry.

I hear the sounds of cars coming, the slam of closing doors, motors revving and the band starting up, the staccato beat of the drums, the shrill voices of girls and the boom of the MC at the microphone. I make my way from the oval to the boys' toilets and sluice my face with water till the redness goes and my eyes clear.

I find the back door to the hall and go in through it and circle up the short run of stairs to the stage. I busy myself with the coils of leads to the amplifiers and pretend I'm working till my mood lifts and my spirits lighten. I head back down the stairs to the auditorium and meet Mr Cassidy, my English teacher, who introduces me to his young wife. 'This is Stephen Bisley, who was Romeo in our production of *Romeo and Juliet* earlier this year.'

'I saw you,' she says. 'It must have been quite a challenge.'

'Yeah, it was,' I reply. She doesn't know the half of it. I wish I had a sword right now. I excuse myself and head through the bodies to the tables of food and drink.

'What'll you have, Stevie?' asks one of the mums and I go for a sausage roll and a cup of cordial.

Dicky Dunn appears at my elbow and whispers, 'Don't drink that shit, mate, have some of this – it'll put hairs on your balls.' He offers me a large bottle of Coke.

I lift it and smell the bourbon way before it gets to my mouth. 'Jesus, how much Coke's in this?'

'Not a whole lot. Get it into ya.' His breath smells like new compost.

'Maybe later,' I say. 'You should take it easy, mate – the prefects are around and they're looking for anyone drinking.'

Nothing's going to deter Dicky though, and he heads off to find another accomplice. I finish my food and I'm ready for a dance. I drape my suit coat over the back of a chair and move out into the heat of the dance floor. There's a group of girls from my class, just milling around together, and I drift over to join them.

'Hey, it's Bizo! You gunna dance?'

'Where's all ya mates?'

It's always the same, has been at every school dance I've ever been to. The girls out on the floor, shuffling around together, ready and willing, and further out in the half light, the boys, puffed up and strutting, all steak and no sizzle, waiting for something to happen, for someone to go.

Tonight it's me, and I don't care, I've got nothing to lose, and no one to lose it with. I'm doing the best I can as the one bloke with a dozen girls, till the band launches into Chuck Berry's 'Johnny B. Goode' – oh, yeah, mama! This is the song that can get the dead up and dancing and I defy anyone with two good legs to sit still when this number is playing. Now they're coming like lemmings over a cliff and the band, sensing the tide is changing, really cranks it up. The lead guitarist is pulling major licks and by the time he hits the first guitar solo the hall is rocking.

All the girls in my group get swept up in an instant and this party has started, one rock'n'roll number hammers into the next and the next, the teachers on the edges, dancing like dorks. Now the band's got us where it wants us as they launch into the Rolling Stones' 'Satisfaction', with the lead singer wailing and the drums crashing. Ties get loosened, shoes kicked off, the heat is rising till the final riff has everyone dripping with sweat.

The band takes a break. I head out the back door for some air. I'm sitting on the top step of the concrete stairs that lead down to the car park when Dicky Dunn finds me again and crashes down beside me.

'How the fuck are ya, Bizo?' He's slurring badly and the Coke bottle's almost empty. His breath smells of recent vomit.

'I'm good, mate, all good. How you doing? Got a job lined up yet?'

'Job? Yeah, nah, yeah. The old man wants me to work with him on the concreting, but ya know something? What I really want to do – like you'll never guess what it is, so don't even try, right – ya know what I really want to do is I wanna join the army. I just wanna shoot someone, ya know? I just wanna shoot the fuck out of the Viet Cong before they get here and take all our good jobs, right? The old man reckons they'll be here doing all the concreting jobs within the next five years. They'll do it because they only get a dollar eighty a year in wages and they can live in a tree, Bizo, a fucking tree. Ya know what I mean, don't ya, Bizo?'

'Yeah, Dicky, I know what you mean, mate, and good luck with it.'

'Hey, Bizo, you wanna joint, mate? Jonesey's got some gear and they're rolling one down behind the ag shed. I'm going there now – wanna come?' With that he's on his feet and moving.

'I might see ya down there, mate. I'm going for a leak.'

'Pooftah!' he yells and disappears into the gloom.

I head back in to the heat and noise of the hall to see what's happening. Suddenly I see her. Susan. She is standing in a group with Brooksey close beside her. I'm okay about it now, I've let the pain go, released her – not that she was ever mine to let go. Would have, could have, should have.

I see Brooksey catch me looking and he whispers something in Susan's ear. She breaks away from the group and walks through the wide front doors into the night. Now he's heading towards me through the crowd but I'm not ready to hear whatever it is he has to say to me and I head out through the back door and make my way to the boys' toilets.

I'm at the urinal when he joins me and unzips. I've known him since we were knee high. We've been as close as brothers without the ties of blood, and friends through everything.

'How's your night?' he asks.

'Yeah, good mate, all good. How's Susan?' I manage to ask.

'She's good, she wants to go, so I'm going to run her home – but I'm coming back, so make sure you're here when I do, 'cause you and I are gunna party.'

Something shifts. I zip and head to the basins.

'Why's she going?'

He joins me at the sink. No answer, just the sound of water.

'Why's she going home? It's only nine-thirty.'

He looks at me.

'You know something, Bizo? Sometimes you need your arse kicked, you know that?'

'What are you talking about?'

'She's going home because she thinks you're not interested in her. The only reason she's here is because of you.'

'I thought you and her were …'

'Me and Susan? Give it a break, mate, she's my cousin. Even if I was interested in her, there's a law against that sort of thing – except in certain states in America, where it's compulsory. I've got an idea: why don't you go and try to get her to stay? She's waiting out by my car. Here's the keys. You know the dirt track that leads up to the dam? If I was you I'd take her for a spin up there and show her the view, the one outside the car. Make sure you're back by twelve, but, 'cause I gotta be home by one. Two prizes in one week. You're doing all right, mate; you're doing just fine.' He drops the car keys into my hand, grins at me for too long, and leaves.

I found her at the car.

Susan and I didn't see a lot of the dam. We saw a lot of each other, though.

I finally got home at three am. Brooksey was too pissed to drive so I hitchhiked and got a lift with a paper truck going north. I was in the laundry, trying to get one of my shoes off in the dark and thinking I was being quiet about it, when suddenly the bare bulb above my head flicked on and Dad was at the door in a blue dressing gown.

I drop the bomb.

'We've never had a father-and-son relationship,' I say as calmly as I can manage.

I wait.

He turns and leaves.

The damage done.

Celibacy

Not long after I finished my exams I applied for a job. I'd seen it in the employment section of the *Sydney Morning Herald* and it had my name written all over it. It was a cadetship in the advertising department of Woolworths' head office in Sydney, just opposite the Town Hall.

The applicant was to be trained as a graphic artist and would be required to attend technical college two nights a week. I had done advanced art at school and thought I would be qualified. I talked it over with my parents and got their approval. I wrote the letter of application with help from Mum and included some examples of my work along with my exam results. It was the first week of November 1966, a month before my sixteenth birthday. A week later I received a reply asking me to attend an interview in Sydney on the Monday of the following week. We arranged for me to stay at Gran's place in Epping. I had made up my mind to live in Sydney and now it felt like a door was creaking open.

    I left on the train on Saturday morning.

I'm on the train with my life in a suitcase. Mum had taken me shopping and I had new slacks. I also had a summer-weight sports coat, which meant it was lightweight. It was so lightweight you could shoot peas through the fabric. Slacks and a summer-weight sports coat. I had two new white shirts, cufflinks, a thin red tie and new shoes by Julius Marlow that pinched a bit when I walked. I had a jar of Brylcreem and three hankies still in the box, socks, undies, two combs, a mouth organ in the key of D and a book by James Joyce. I had a new wallet given to me last Christmas which until this morning had still been in the box. I had a condom in the corner of the wallet, which made a perfect circle shape through the leather, and although I hadn't really had sex it made me look like an experienced lover, a Casanova, a scoundrel. Whenever I got the wallet out I made sure I placed it circle side up in the hope that it might attract some loose women.

The compartment I was in had two long padded seats between the window and the sliding door which led to the passageway that ran the entire length of the carriage. I left the sliding door open with my wallet beside me on the seat, circle side up, in case there were any loose women riding the train looking for love with a stranger. We hadn't left the station yet but, as always, I was fairly optimistic.

I could see how it might happen. Some haunted blonde, running from a drug-crazed husband and a troubled past, would lurch down the passageway, steady herself at the open door of my compartment and see me through the tears of regret. She would dab at the corners of her almond-shaped eyes with an exquisite silk handkerchief, her breasts straining at the thin fabric of her blouse, her fishnet stockings spidering across her long legs. Then, gathering herself, she would step through the door and into my life.

The blonde eased herself into the vacant seat opposite me. I felt her eyes on me, all over me. Then they shifted and she let them drift down my perfectly ironed slacks to the wallet on the seat beside me. The wallet with the perfect circle etched into the fine grain of the leather. Her eyes lingered and she got the message loud and clear. Her red lips parted and the corners of her mouth curled into a smile. I flicked my blues up from the magazine and hit her with the high beam. My look said, 'Maybe?'

I drifted back to the magazine and the article on whale blubber and its dietary importance to the Eskimos, knowing that it was just a matter of time, and time was something I never wasted. Never.

Her next move came sooner than I expected. She unfolded those long legs and walked to the compartment door, slid it closed and locked it tight, real tight. I reached for the packet of Luckies in the breast pocket of my lightweight sports jacket, flipped one between my moist lips and torched it with the Zippo. I felt her fingers on my slacks, tracing the razor edge of the crease, higher and higher till finally she found my – 'All change at Gosford for the Sydney train on platform two! Hey, mate, got yer ticket there for me?'

I woke up to find the conductor shaking me. I looked at him blankly.

'Ticket, please! Ticket?'

I was on a train, yes, Sydney, ticket.

'Sorry, um ...'

I fumbled for my wallet and remembered it was on the seat beside me. I opened it, still clumsy with sleep. The condom fell on the floor and landed beside one of his square black shoes.

'Bit young to be packing one of those, aren't ya? I'd put it away, if I was you, and give it back to your dad when you get home.'

How did he know I'd nicked it? Did he know about the white box? Did he know Dad?

I found the ticket and offered it to him.

'Well, this train terminates here and the Sydney train leaves from platform two in twenty minutes. Better not leave that lying there either – might fall into the wrong hands. Might end up with somebody who actually knows how to use it, eh?'

I bought a cheese and pickle sandwich from the kiosk on the platform and, when I'd finished it, I stood behind a potted shrub and eased the condom out of my wallet. I wrapped it in the brown paper bag that the sandwich had come in and when I was sure the coast was clear I placed it deep inside a rubbish bin. Then I made my way to platform two, a reformed and celibate man.

Gran's house

I love Gran's house – it's warm and welcoming, just like Gran. She meets me at the door and hugs me close. The smell of lavender and powder wraps around me.

She shows me to the spare room, which has a huge bed with a deep mattress and soft pillows. More lavender scent drifts in through the open windows. I unpack my small suitcase, putting the harmonica on the bedside table along with the book by James Joyce. Home away from home. I've never played the harmonica or read anything by James Joyce, but I plan to do both things sometime soon. I really don't know why I brought them with me. They just looked good together in the suitcase. I hang the slacks and the lightweight sports coat in the wardrobe, change into my shorts and T-shirt and join Gran in the kitchen for a cuppa and thick sandwiches.

Gran's going to bingo tonight and wants to know if I'd like to come. The thought of a few hours in a dusty hall with a lot of old people is hard to turn down, but I do, reluctantly. I want to go to Kings Cross. I've heard all the rumours and I want to find out if they're true. I don't want to alarm Gran so I tell her I'm meeting a friend in town to go to the movies. Of course, she doesn't know that I don't have any friends in Sydney – except Susan, but I'm meeting her tomorrow.

I've never seen anything like it. I catch the train to the city and walk up William Street. There are scantily clad women on every corner. Chicks in see-through tops with their breasts on show for all to see. 'Wanna go, love?' offers one; she's as old as one of my aunties. I don't know where to look, but I look anyway. I've only ever played this sort of thing out in my head. I had no idea that it happened in the real world! You could just walk along here and get a girl right off the street and just … I stood there totally transfixed, feeling like some dumb country bumpkin.

There are cars crawling along William Street, stopping at all the girls, till finally the door opens and a girl gets in to be spirited away into the night. How long had this been going on?

Towards the top of the hill I notice a group of men in one of the side streets and decide to see what's happening. They're all just standing around, dozens of them, outside a small single-storey terrace house with a red light by the open front door. There's a chair in the hall just back from the door. On the chair sits a blonde of ample proportions, bare-breasted beneath her see-through top. She is the girl of my dreams. A guy walks through the front gate, into the yard and up to the door. A short conversation takes place and the front door closes.

I walk further along the street. There are dozens of houses with red lights and girls of all shapes and sizes, the front doors opening and closing, while a stream of men comes and goes. No pun intended, because I'm only fifteen and don't know what a pun is yet, but I will shortly. I think I've bitten off more than I can chew and I'm not sure whether it's wise to be here by myself. I think I should have gone to bingo with Gran, where the only trouble you can get into is forgetting to turn your hearing aid on before they start calling out the numbers.

I head back to the safety of the bright lights of William Street and continue up the hill to Kings Cross. Now I'm right in the heart of it. There are people everywhere and it seems like every crazy person living in Sydney has decided to come here tonight. It's weirder than the sideshow alley at the Wyong Show. There are more girls up here. There are girls that look like men and men that look like girls and other people who look like a bit of both.

There's a man sitting on the footpath with people milling all around him. He has a dog sitting beside him. The man looks sad, the dog looks sadder. No one seems to notice them. The man has a sign drawn on a piece of old cardboard beside a battered tin cup. The sign says CAN YOU SPARE SOME CHANGE FOR FOOD. I've never seen a beggar before. Nobody ever begs for food in Lake Munmorah. I get the new wallet out. I extract a dollar note and then another one. It's the money I've earnt from fruit picking. I put the two single dollar notes into the cup. I want to tell him about Lake Munmorah and all the fruit trees. If he lived there he'd never go hungry. There's always enough to go around for everyone and it would be a better life for the dog. He doesn't say thank you, so I just move on. The dog watches me go.

I put the wallet in the front pocket of my pants just to keep it safe. I only get a few paces along the street when I decide to go back; I want to make sure that the man understands that one of the dollars is for him and that the other one is for the dog. But when I get there the sad guy's gone and so has the cup. The dog's still there though. I try to pat it, but it growls at me and nips my hand. I push on. Further along a man steps out from nowhere and puts his hand in the middle of my chest. He has long straggly hair. The word *hate* is tattooed across the fingers of the hand on my chest. 'Wanna look?' he asks. He smiles and bits of gold flash behind the grin.

'Sorry?'

'Downstairs, mate, ten beautiful girls, they'll get their gear off just for you, only five bucks.' The place is called the Pink Pussycat and it has a notice by the front door that reads *Only people over the age of eighteen will be admitted to these premises.* I do want to go for a look – maybe Lolita from the tent at the Wyong Show has given up life on the road and is down there taking her clothes off for other men – but I'm a changed man now, focused and determined.

'No thanks,' I say.

'All right, two bucks then – but don't tell anyone, will ya?'

I walk on, wondering how focused and determined I really am.

More girls line the walls between the shops, all with the same hollow look as the ones on William Street. There's a bloke at the back of a small van singing songs about Jesus. He has a guitar and a tambourine. I once saw a Salvation Army band in Newcastle singing songs about Jesus. One of the girls in the band had a tambourine as well. Maybe it's a Jesus thing. Maybe Jesus played a tambourine. I don't think I've ever read anything about what sort of musical instrument Jesus played. The long hair and the beard suggest to me that it might have been the bongos or maybe a guitar.

Further along there's a bloke sitting on a stool in front of a shop that's closed and dark. He's playing a violin with a white cockatoo perched on the end of his bow. As he draws the bow across the strings the bird dances back and forth in time to the music. He's doing much better business than the guy with the sad dog. It seems all you need to make money around here is an animal of some sort, a tin cup and a sign and you're in business. Maybe I could bring Dukey the dog down. Maybe I could work up an act with Dukey the dog, my brother and a stock whip. It could be a hit.

I've come to the end of the strip and I don't know what else to do. I decide to head back to Gran's. I push through the crowds to find a bus stop. I pass the spot with the bloke and the dog. The bloke's back. He's drinking out of a bottle that's sticking out of a brown paper bag. I hope the dog got some food, but I doubt it.

It takes an hour to get back to Gran's. I let myself in to the quiet house and find my bedroom in the dark as the grandfather clock chimes twelve. I lie in the big bed and wonder what Mum's doing at home. I wonder if she misses me. I wonder if Dad's sitting on the end of the bed, counting his condoms. I wonder.

Bliss

I'm standing in front of the Sydney Town Hall waiting for Susan to arrive. It's nine o'clock on Sunday morning. Tomorrow morning, at another nine o'clock, I'm having my interview on the fourth floor of the Woolworths building directly opposite where I'm standing.

I hear a car horn blaring. It's Susan, waving frantically at me from a car pulled up at the kerb. I run to the car and get in.

'What's this? I thought you were coming by train – I didn't even know you could drive!'

She makes a right-hand turn into Park Street.

'It's my dad's car. It'll be easier to get around this way. I want to take you to Bondi, to the beach. I've borrowed a pair of my brother's swimmers for you; you're about the same size – and if they don't fit you'll just have to go in nude, won't you?'

We are heading up William Street now.

'I was here last night, at the Cross – the place is a hole,' I say.

'Did you find a girl you liked?' she asks.

'Already got one,' I reply.

I reach over and take her free hand in mine and she squeezes mine back.

'Do you remember when you got on my bus on the last day of primary school?' she asks.

'Sure do,' I say.

'Do you remember what you said to me?'

'Yep.'

She is smiling that smile again, with her blue eyes darting between me and the road.

'What was it then?' she challenges.

'I said you were the ugliest chick I had ever seen!'

She lets go of my hand and punches me in the upper arm. 'No, seriously,' she says. 'I want to know if you remember.'

I know it's important to her, it's a bit of a test I think; she wants to know if I really care. 'I said: I like you.'

She swerves to the side of the road and stops the car, and before I know it she's got my head in her hands and she is kissing me long and hard. When she finally releases me she looks at me for a long moment, then says, 'I want to show you something.' She reaches over to the back seat for her beach bag and puts it into the space between us. She gently unfolds a beach towel from the top of the bag and nestled inside it is a small brown paper bag. Inside the bag is the makeup I gave her almost four years ago.

I am with one hell of an amazing girl – and you know what? She's a brunette!

Bondi is tops. I'm in her brother's swimmers that actually fit and we're in the surf with about a million other people. How cool is this, a surf beach in the middle of the city? Susan is in a bikini and I can't take my eyes off her. She holds me close to her, the cool water running between us, which is a godsend. We are going to head back to our towels but I have to swim away from her first, away from the closeness of her, to settle myself down before I can leave the water; it's a boy thing. On the towels we kiss for hours and explore each other. I want more of her but she says we can't, so we don't. I wish I could play hard to get, but it seems out of the realm of possibility.

We stay at the beach all day, and have fish and chips out of a box. We walk on the sand hand in hand and talk our lives out till the shadows grow long on the beach and we have to go. She drives me home and meets Gran and I can hardly bear it when she leaves.

A wanted man

It's nine am. I'm sitting in the reception area on the fourth floor of Woolworths' head office and I want to be sick. The room is full of guys my age. I am the worst-dressed person in the room by far. I look like I've been dressed by St Vincent de Paul. There are guys in body shirts and velvet jackets with high-waisted bellbottom pants. Some with paisley shirts and scarves knotted at their throats. Elegant three-piece suits with brightly coloured silk ties. There's a guy with a full-length leather coat and a floppy black hat. They all look like they've just come from a fashion shoot in Swinging London. I look like one of the men who follows the cows around with a shovel at the Wyong Show. What was I thinking? I looked all right at home in the long mirror in Mum's bedroom in Lake Munmorah, the style capital of the universe. Maybe I should leave now, catch the next train home and put my name down at the power station. This is not for me. This is for cool people, people with style.

I leaf through the samples of work I have in a folder on my lap, just to look busy. The power station won't be so bad; at least I'll know people there. Maybe I could take over the farm and grow tomatoes. Maybe I'll ask Susan to marry me tonight and we can build a small house, well away from my parents' place, maybe on the edge of the creek, and she can have the kids while I work at the power station and grow tomatoes, and when they're old enough I can bundle them into an old truck and take them to the markets in Newcastle, the kids and the tomatoes.

'Stephen Bisley?' It's the receptionist.

'That's me,' I say, rising to my feet.

She steps out from behind her desk. All eyes in the room are on me, just for the fashion tips obviously.

'Follow me, please.'

She leads me down a corridor. She looks great from behind, if only I didn't already have a girlfriend! I just realised it, right here this second: I am going steady! It's such a great thing to say!

We've arrived at a large open area. There are people working at drafting tables, others at light boxes, some at conventional desks. Everyone is busy and I love the energy of the place. I don't really want to work at the power station.

'Stephen?' There's a guy standing in front of me with his hand outstretched. His handshake feels firm and warm and equal. 'I'm Karl. Wanna walk this way?' He shows me into one of the offices to the side of the open-plan area, and closes the door behind us.

'Take a seat,' he says as he moves to sit behind the desk. 'So you're down from beautiful Lake Munmorah?'

I like him already; he has a great sense of humour. I can't help but smile.

'No, I'm serious, I love it up there! My wife's parents have a place on the lake. So, you went to Wyong High?'

I nod. Having Wyong High and Lake Munmorah on the top of your CV is maybe not the best way to get your foot in the door.

'Stephen, I really like the samples you sent me with the application. What I'd like to do now is to put you in one of the studios and have you draw something for us. The main area we work in is advertisements, particularly for newspapers. So I'll get Lisa, one of our artists, to look after you. Sorry to make our meeting so brief, but as you probably saw in the reception area I have a few people to see today. Nice to have met you.' He shakes my hand again and leaves. Even if I don't get the job it was so great to be treated like that. What a guy! Maybe it's an advertising thing, make the first impression a lasting one; well, it's worked on me.

I meet Lisa and she takes me into one of the vacant studios. There is a drafting table with a large piece of white paper pinned to it. Next to the blank sheet are some newspaper clippings with pictures of different items of merchandise drawn on them. Beside the table is a pair of men's running shoes, one balanced artistically on the other.

'Okay, Stephen, it's pretty straightforward. Have a look at some of the ads, which will give you an idea of the style we use around here, then have a go at drawing the shoes. If you need anything, I'll be in the studio next door. Good luck.' And she smiles and leaves.

I'm an artist. It doesn't matter what my clothes look like or where I'm from. I'm sitting in an artist's studio in the middle of Sydney. If I was struck by lightning right now I would die a happy man. I look out through the open door of the studio and see other artists working in the room. If I don't get this job I want to remember this moment forever.

I get to work. I draw the shoes three times, each one a little different from the other. I don't know how long I'm meant to take, but I'm finished in half an hour, so I go looking for Lisa. She's next door with lots of samples of bras piled on her desk.

'Sorry about the mess; we're having a sale next week and I've being drawing these for days. How'd you go?'

'Okay, I hope,' I say.

'Karl wanted me to tell you that they'll be making a decision by lunchtime today, so if you want to leave your home phone number with the receptionist, they'll give you a call later.'

'Would it be all right if I came back this afternoon to find out?' I'm trying not to sound desperate.

'I'm sure that would be fine. Why don't you come at two?'

Lisa walks me back to the reception area. I deflate a bit when I see the fashion crew again and they all give me the once-over as I leave – but you can't judge a book by its cover, as Mum would say. I head north up George Street towards the harbour.

At quarter to two I am back. I stand on the footpath outside Woolworths, reluctant to go inside. I am afraid of rejection, of having to go home a failure. It feels like my whole future is riding on the results of this one day.

On the dot of two I enter the building. When I reach the fourth floor I take a deep breath and open the door to the reception area. There is no one waiting this time. The receptionist is on the phone. I sit on the edge of a chair and wait. She takes two more calls. I wait. She finally hangs up the phone and I approach her desk. She looks up.

'Can I help you?' she asks, without a smile.

'I was told to come back at two to find out whether I was successful in my job application. I had an interview this morning with Karl.'

'Just hold on a moment.' She dials an extension on the phone. 'I've got a guy here who says he was asked to call back this afternoon, something about a job …' She covers the mouthpiece with her free hand. 'What was your name, sorry?'

'Steve,' I reply. 'Steve Bisley.'

'Steve Bisley,' she says into the phone. 'Okay, I'll tell him.'

Here it comes, the blow.

'Karl will come and talk to you. Just take a seat, he won't be long.' And she answers another call.

I go back to my seat. I wait.

A few minutes later Karl comes down the corridor. I stand ready for the blow. He stops in front of me.

'Steve, thanks for coming back, but I have some bad news, I'm afraid.'

Tears spring to the back of my eyes, and it takes everything I have to hold them there and not let them spill. 'The bad news is this: none of the other guys got the job – but you did, so congratulations!'

His hand is outstretched again and I grab it too hard and now the tears are welling up and there is nothing I can do about it.

'You okay? I'm sorry – that was a rotten thing to do to you.'

'I'm fine,' I blurt. 'And thank you, thank you so much.' I pump his hand again.

'All right. Now we'd like you to start on January the third; that will let you have Christmas at home. We'll send all the info to your home address in the next day or so. If you need to ask me anything, here's my card. So once again, congratulations, Steve, and we'll see you in the New Year.' With that he leaves. I slide his card into my new wallet.

I've got a job, I've got a future … I feel like I could burst.

Changes

I was home, but only for a month. Only a month till I started my new life. It seems strange to me. I'm only just coming to terms with my old one. Things were changing so fast. The end of so many things and the beginning of others. I've only been back home a week and already it's started.

Fish's dad died while I was away. It was a Saturday and Fish had gone to his job at the pharmacy. The pub had opened at ten as usual and the barman had poured his dad's first white wine of the day, like he'd done for as long as he could remember. When he hadn't turned up by three minutes past, the barman knew something was wrong and called Fish at work. Fish rushed home and found his father. It wasn't the booze that had killed him; he'd hanged himself in the garage. He'd stood on the stool that Fish had salvaged for him from the tip. There was no note. I went to the funeral. There was no other family there, just Fish, and his mates who loved him. Everyone from the pub was there. It must have been a black day for them, losing their best customer. Fish had tried to get in touch with his mum, to let her know what had happened, but nobody knew where she was. We weren't legally old enough to drink but we had our own private wake in a back room at the pub. The owner put a keg on for free and left us to it. Fish's old man would have loved it. I guess dying was the only way he was ever going to get sober.

I stay at Fish's place that night in the hammock on the front verandah because he didn't want me to come inside. A lot of people offered to take him in and look after him but he'd battled his whole life to stay in his own home and he wasn't going to change now.

I didn't see him after I moved to Sydney but I heard he'd gone back to school, got his Leaving Certificate and was accepted into Sydney University, where he studied to become a pharmacist.

I got a job offsiding with a local builder. I needed to earn some money before my job started in early January. Alf was amazing to watch. He had these big square hands that were gnarly and calloused. He was well into his sixties and he was tireless. We'd do a twelve-hour day and I'd be buggered at the end of it, while Alf looked as fresh as when we'd started. He could do anything with a stick of timber. He'd been in the building trade since he was just a kid, working with his old man. That was back in the 1920s, when new towns were springing up everywhere. Alf and his dad travelled in an old truck with all the tools they needed on the back. They only ever built hotels, the big old ones you see on the street corners of every country town. They'd arrive in town and start building the whole pub – the bars downstairs, the giant wooden staircases, the rooms upstairs. Sometimes they'd be in town for a year. And when they finished they'd be off to the next place to do it all again. These days he was living locally and doing mostly restorations and additions to residential properties.

We were putting a deck on a house on the shores of the lake. One day Dicky Dunn and his old man turned up to do the concreting on a new driveway. When we broke for lunch, Dicky and I took our sandwiches down to the water. We'd just sat down when the big siren sounded the shift change from the power station.

'Julie's pregnant,' he said in the following quiet.

More changes. Julie was Dicky's on-and-off girlfriend. More off than on. It was a stormy relationship to say the least. She'd left school two years ago when she was fifteen, and they'd started going out soon after. She worked at one of the two hairdressing salons in town.

'What are you going to do?' I asked.

'I'm going into the army, mate; had the interview a week ago. I go two weeks after Christmas. Hope I get to go to 'Nam – I'll shoot a couple of gooks for you, mate.'

'What's going to happen with the baby, Dicky?'

'She wants to keep it,' he said. 'So does her mum.'

'What do *you* want, mate?' I asked.

'I don't give a fuck, mate, I'll be in Vietnam. She can do what she likes!'

I sipped the milky tea from my thermos and looked across the wide expanse of the lake. I remembered Dicky at the show with the love bites on his neck, scaring the shit out of people on the ghost train for five bob an hour and knew that

that was the best time of our lives. I was still fifteen, Dicky only a year older, and we shouldn't have been having this conversation. It was so wrong.

'Have you told your folks yet?'

'Yeah,' he said. 'Mum had a yarn to her, told her to get rid of it, and Dad called me a fuckwit – still won't look at me.' A silver fish jumps on the silent lake. 'Hey, listen Bizo, let's go to the pub Saturday night? I know the bloke on the door, won't be a problem.'

With Dicky, nothing would ever be a problem.

'I've got to get back, mate.'

'Sure,' he said and we headed to the house.

Later, as we're packing up, I watch Dicky with his silent father trowelling the last of the driveway, his future set just like the concrete.

Christmas

When I was a little kid I would put carrots out on the verandah for the reindeer, and cake and milk for Santa. On Christmas Eve I would sit out there, looking out over the dark paddocks, waiting for the twinkling lights of the sled to come till sleep claimed me and I missed him again. One Christmas morning I found the carrots undisturbed where I had left them and the milk and cake untouched. I didn't tell anyone but it troubled me.

I believed in Santa Claus. Even when I found a cache of unwrapped presents in the linen press that ended up under the tree wrapped in bright paper with swing tags that read 'To Stevie, From Santa'. I asked Mum about it and she told me that Santa had delivered them early because he had run out of wrapping paper and had asked my mother, if it wasn't too much trouble, if she could wrap them on his behalf this year. My mother had agreed only after an assurance from Santa that it would never happen again. My mother could be firm when it was required. I believed every word of it.

Back then I also thought that Santa and Christ were somehow linked, a dynamic duo, a bit like Batman and Robin. I can remember standing at the front of a department store in Newcastle staring at a nativity scene. In one window was the manger with a small bed lined with straw. In the straw lay the baby Jesus with a few cows and some sheep in attendance. In the very next window was Santa's workshop with a lot of busy elves getting the presents organised for Santa to deliver. I think this is where the confusion began. For years I thought that Jesus rode around with Santa in the sled and helped him deliver the presents. This was the only miracle I ever believed in.

And now it's another Christmas morning. Too hot, too early, airless and still. The grass is browning on the lawn and the big gum trees are sagging. The dog hasn't left the cool of the laundry slab in a week. I slept under a single sheet last night, but even that was too much and I woke up this morning hot and clammy.

The Christmas tree in the corner next to the TV has gone all brittle in the heat and doesn't smell alpine anymore. There are cards on the mantelpiece above the oil heater, where the open fire used to be. The cards have pictures of snow on them. A snowman, a house in the snow, children playing in the snow, Santa with his sled full of presents in the snow.

I wrapped my presents last night and they're stacked under the tree. I bought Dad an electric razor last year knowing that he is strictly a blade man. He's never taken it out of the box, so this year I've got him another one. Mum's easy to buy for, slippers and perfume. There's a shirt in a box for my brother, some perfume for his new wife and a Bob Dylan album for Kris.

The house is quiet, just the sound of the fridge groaning from the kitchen. I'm the only kid left in the house. My brother's married now and living in another fibro house down by the lake and my sister will come from Newcastle later this morning. The sun's barely above the tree line and already the paddocks are crackling like cellophane. I unwind myself from the sheet and make my way outside in the hope there might be some early breeze but the big gums are still and nothing is moving.

I sit on the edge of the verandah. The kookaburras start their chorus but this morning even they're a bit half-hearted. The one cow is lying under the shade of the one tree in the paddock. I hear Mum in the kitchen and the kettle whistling and the sound of a spoon in a cup. She's out through the screen door now with two steaming cups and she perches beside me.

'Having a last look?' she asks, knowing me too well.

'Yeah, last look.' And we sit in the quiet, just me and Mum. We sit till the last of our tea is gone and she says, 'Well, this won't buy the baby a rug,' and I know it's a call to action, that we're up and into the day. I head for the bathroom and a shower and she's in the kitchen clearing the decks.

An hour later we've stuffed the turkey and it's in the oven and it's the start of the Christmas marathon. There's a pudding bubbling away in one pot and thick molten gravy in another. Dad's sharpening the knives for carving and getting in everyone's way. Bing Crosby's crooning on the record player about a white Christmas somewhere else and the flies are gathered like gangs on the screen door.

Richard and his new wife, Lisabeth, arrive with presents and bright pink prawns and more grog to go with the grog that's already here. Kristin's suddenly through the gate and the dog rouses and wags himself stupid. She's through the door and everyone hugs everyone again, the first wine of the day gets poured and I nick one and nobody cares. There are peanuts in bowls and cashews in others and sugared almonds in even more as well as candied ginger and things you'll never see for another year, but you eat them because they're there and it's Christmas and everything is forgotten and let go.

So Dad plays Santa and hands the presents around and announces who they're from and who they're for, and the paper gets torn to shreds and everyone gets everything they've ever wanted and we sit in new starchy shirts with the pins still in them and someone's got tinsel in their hair and the dog's allowed inside and pisses on the rug in the lounge room from the sheer excitement of it all.

Dad likes the electric razor for a minute and forgets he already has one. Bob Dylan replaces Bing on the record player and the answer my friend is blowing in the wind, but not here, where it must be thirty-something degrees and climbing. Mum's had too many wines already but so has everybody else, and we swarm back to the kitchen and everyone gets in everyone's way and the prawns get peeled and the table gets laid with Mum's best things and the turkey gets hauled from the oven and Dad's all over it with the bright knives. Richard's carving the ham and piles of baked potatoes tumble on the waiting platters with the other root vegetables, and the molten gravy goes into a delicate china jug that once belonged to Nan before she became a chicken and we plonk down around the groaning table and pull bonbons with whoever's closest and we all cheer at the bang and put the stupid paper hats on.

Mum's best plates get piled with too much of everything and we eat and talk and eat like refugees and drink everything that's open and open more and drink that till everything is forgotten and we laugh at things that were never funny and never will be but are today and that's the only thing that matters. The frenzy continues through the steaming pudding with the thrupenny bits and the orange peel and glacé cherries and the dense dried fruit and the sweet custard that gulps from the jug.

We heave ourselves from the table and collapse into the lounge room with the lethargy of over-indulgence to drink more and then some more until the conversations falter and peter out and everyone heads to the waiting beds to collapse and sleep like lizards in the sun.

Later when the house has cooled we drift from the fug of sleep to the last light of the day on the edge of the verandah. We sit in the quiet of the last of Christmas suddenly like a family together, but alone in the still evening with our thoughts slithering back and further back. Later we curl up with new books or sit together with bits of things to say, until the talk becomes awkward and things get packed and there's talk of the need to go and the last bus to Newcastle if I'm quick and thanks for everything and thanks for coming and Mum says 'Mind how you go' to everyone except me and Dad, who are staying.

I get two more presents because in a few hours I'll be sixteen and I'll eat ham tomorrow to celebrate. Richard will drop Kris at the last bus to Newcastle so they're all in the car now with Lisabeth in the front seat smiling and then they're gone, past the swinging gate and under the canopy of bright stars, to their new homes.

Epilogue

I waited till my parents were through the screen door and I swung on the big gate till it slammed into the stout corner post and made my teeth rattle.

I sat in the night for a long time.

A new moon rose above the dark gums and turned the paddocks all to silver.

I had always loved the farm in the dark. Things at peace and resting after the coarse brightness of the day. Things stark and defined.

I walked the track to the creek and stood beside the pump-house shed. I looked back toward the house, to other times.

To three children, their faces lamp-lit and golden, like small treasures huddled together in the warmth. The bright fire crackling in the dark house. Wood smoke curling from the chimney. My mother weaving stories of wonder in the glow.

My parents' hands entwined across the kitchen table, their love unbridled and new.

To later, and the scissored willow in the corner of the yard, the dark innards of the shed and the start of broken bits, of drowned things.

I dreamed a waking dream, of my father walking the track between the two paddocks. There is no sack in his hands. His palms are open and his arms outstretched. He is smiling. I run toward him through the silver-edged night. He claims me, close, his strong arms encircle me and he holds me like something precious. His breath warm against my face, his lips as tender as a first kiss as the stars fall to earth around us and I hold the only gift I ever wanted, the one I never had – my father's love.

I start for the house, the stars still in their places above me. Things as they were and always will be, unchanged and set.

Tomorrow I'll walk the thousand steps to the blue-black highway.

A thousand steps to freedom and life.

And a world away from a paddock of sticks.

Mum's poems

Mum is the reason I was able to write this book. She taught me about the music of words.

Mum wrote poems all the time at home. The beauty of them makes me weep whenever I read them. I remember telling her once that she should have them published.

I can now make that happen. Here are just a few of many.

Thanks Mum.

END OF WINTER LETTER

Gathered like question marks

On the edge of the bay

The black swans ask about the imminence of spring.

And in the river

Seventeen great white herons

Mirrored in silver paper water

Are flanked by a postscript

Of busy black ducks.

POEM AT HOME

At home there is only a battalion of small things
Which march up and down my days.
Washing on the line,
Leaves on the lawn,
Cup on the table betokening tea.
Black smelly beetles on the lemon tree
Dust in corners awaiting a broom
A long legged spider spinning his loom
Unanswered letters in a rack,
Crying 'Please Write Back'.
So I go forth to the garden
Where I found and lost my love.

PRETTY SPRING DAY

There was just
That calm and lovely morning,
Wind dropped from yesterday's ferment,
Stepping to the green grass's invitation,
I flung orange peels to the cows,
Looked up to the blue, blue sky
And little darling clouds
Like feathers or fish bones, but white
As babies' eyeballs.
There were scents;
Pittosporum's heavy-laden breath;
The faint whisper of wisteria
And the old nostalgia of clover.
Bees nosed the poppies' bright banners,
Peered into pansies' monkey faces,
Touched lightly the pungent marguerites,
Drank deep of purple stocks
And sated, flew away.

Two rosellas

Sat in the willow's scanty arms

While the mickey miner mother kept her babies from
    the cat.

Kookaburras' neat heads disarrayed in the breeze

And a wagtail proclaimed his love.

While you and I,

Old blood rising like yeast

Smiled at each other and remembered –

Other Springs.

KRISSIE'S PEAR TREE

She found it in the bush

Brought it home

Imperious with ownership.

It must be planted just there

Where she dug a hole

Right by the clothes line.

They all said 'What is it?'

She answered with five-year-old certainty

'A pear tree.

It will have yellow pears.'

Twenty years it took

To blossom and she had gone

To sow her own life's orchard –

Some of her tree bloomed early

Had little fruit, and withered young.

Her pear tree now, gnarling –

Putting out beseeching blossom –

Remembering that small hand,

Says – 'I renew and may have yellow pears.'

Acknowledgements

The readers and the listeners

To Peter Fisher who was always there for me, who was my constant reader and gave me hope and laughed in all the right places, went quiet in the other bits and never spilt beer on the manuscript. To Trudy Billsbury who has way too much love inside her for one person and listened and read. To my soulmate Stephen Broomhall for the well-trodden welcome mat at his door.

Russell Bacon and Sasha Madon for always being there when I arrived at their door with a sheaf of paper in my hand, who always listened and urged me on. Victoria Buchan and Greg Hall, Colin, Louisa and Simon, Tristan, Tara and baby Max for their love and encouragement and food and wine. To my lifetime friend Dee Tipping for everything and more. To Ken Johnson for the beauty he brings to everything. To Annie Markey who smiled that winning smile, hosted a dinner to celebrate the end of the writing journey, and if she doesn't already know how much I love her, then she will now.

To Catherine Milne who mentioned 'walking over broken glass' to work with me on this book, and with her feet swathed in bandages became my publisher. To the unseen, fantastic crew at HarperCollins for all their effort to get my book 'out there'. To my theatrical agent, Sue Barnett, for having the patience of a saint and sticking by me in the tough times.

The Lovers

To my children: Amber, Paris, Jesse, Indiana, Scarlett and Jasper. The only people in my life who have taught me the true meaning of 'unconditional love'.

Thank you.